BASIC AND AD
LIGHT PLANE MAI

Systems Mai

The Light Plane Maintenance Library
Volume Three

BASIC AND ADVANCED
LIGHT PLANE MAINTENANCE

Systems Maintenance

By the Editors of *Light Plane*
Maintenance Magazine

Belvoir Publications Inc.
Riverside, Connecticut 06878

ISBN: 0-9615196-2-2

Please Note: The information appearing in this publication is presented for educational purposes only. In no case shall the publishers be held responsible for any use readers may choose to make (or not to make) of this information. Readers are hereby advised that Federal Aviation Regulation 91.163(a) places primary responsibility for ensuring the airworthy condition of any aircraft on the aircraft owner or operator. Any person who performs inspections, alterations, and/or repairs on any aircraft does so entirely at his or her own risk.

Contents

Preface   vii

Part I: THE PANEL AND RELATED SYSTEMS

Chapter 1:   Into the Panel   3
Working Inside the Panel
The Magnetic Compass
Refashioning the Panel

Chapter 2:   Vacuum and Pitot-Static   31
                System Maintenance
Vacuum Systems and Their Problems
Servicing the Air-Oil Separator
Dry Vacuum Pumps: Failures and Replacement
Handling Filters and Gyro Instruments
Pitot-Static Protection

Chapter 3:   Engine Instruments   55
An Instrument Literacy Challenge
Oil Pressure Gauges
Tachometers
EGT and CHT

Part II: ELECTRICAL EQUIPMENT

Chapter 4:   Under the Wire   89
Survival Tips for Old Radios
Cockpit Speaker Replacement
Troubleshooting a Strobe System
Do-It-Yourself ELT Maintenance
Maintaining Contacts

Chapter 5:   Alternators and Generators   115
Alternators
Keeping Your DC Generator Alive
Generator Troubleshooting
How to Inspect and Maintain a Voltage Regulator

Chapter 6: Batteries   **143**
    Basic Maintenance Procedures
    Replacement and Preservation
    Cold-- and Hot-Weather Maintenance

APPENDICES

Appendix A: Gyro Instrument   **171**
        Troubleshooting
Appendix B: Pitot-Static Instrument   **176**
        Troubleshooting
Appendix C: Manifold Pressure   **180**
        Gauge Troubleshooting
Appendix D: Battery Troubleshooting   **183**

Index   **189**

Preface

It was perhaps an ironic inevitability that as the capabilities of aircraft grew greater, the points of aircraft vulnerability would rest with smaller and smaller items. Today, wings rarely crumble or fall off, and main airframe components display remarkable strength. But the relatively tiny components of the systems by which we navigate, communicate, and monitor the well-being of our airplanes in flight have a disturbing way of blinking out, expensively and at times dangerously.

Many a pilot who has no qualms about whipping his airframe through stressful maneuvers or bouncing it about the runway during graceless landings, may expend a great deal of worry over vacuum pumps, panel switches, radio components, battery terminals, and other devices. And for good reason: When these inventions fail us, they can leave us hanging in mid-cloud with airplanes that are virtually blind or deaf or powerless.

Aircraft owners can perform certain tasks of maintenance related to these areas, *as long as they observe the legalities set forth by the FAA.* It's important to know what you're doing, of course. In fact, even if you, as an owner or pilot, never touch your panel or electrical equipment with intent to perform maintenance, just knowing how such things go wrong and how they can be protected can enable you to recognize danger signs and alert your friendly mechanic to check them out.

Such knowledge is closely related to your confidence as a pilot. We feel that the pilot who can firmly rely on the indications in his cockpit and the systems they describe is bound to be more secure, better motivated, and, therefore, safer as an airman.

As with the first two volumes of The Light Plane Maintenance library, this book is based on materials that have appeared in *Light Plane Maintenance* Magazine. It is intended to serve aviation safety and to enable owners and pilots to get the utmost benefit from their aircraft.

As before, please keep in mind that sources and suppliers for equipment, materials, and services given in this book are as of the first publication of the articles from which these chapters have been adapted. Similarly, we have generally refrained from quoting costs

and prices so as to avoid obsolescence and misinforming our readers. Except where indicated, quoted figures are as of early 1986. We suggest that you consult *Light Plane Maintenance* regularly or contact the firms involved to keep apprised of changes in prices, services, and related matters.

In some discussions, we describe principles and methods through work done on specific aircraft. We do so in the belief that these examples pertain to procedures that are *similar* to those which other owners may be able to follow. We recommend, however, that you resolve any questions or uncertainties you may have by consulting a qualified professional mechanic or an FAA representative. In maintenance as in flying, safety must be the foremost consideration.

Riverside, Connecticut
July 1987

Part I
THE PANEL
AND RELATED SYSTEMS

Chapter 1

INTO THE PANEL

Not only for the IFR ticket holder but for the sunshine pilot as well, the integrity of his or her airplane's instruments may be the key to salvation. We all grow intimately familiar with the faces our instruments show us, but usually our last real acquaintance with the anatomies behind the glass, needles, and numbers was during our student days, when FAA writtens were more on our minds than naked survival. However, it should take but one flight in which an instrument bugs out when it is really needed to raise a truly sentient survivor's gauge-consciousness—or at least his intense curiosity—about the little world beneath the windscreen.

Instrument failures (not vacuum or electrical system failures, but genuine gauge glitches) have always been somewhat rare in aviation, thankfully, though they are not as rare now as in the old AN-gyro days. Today's proliferation of foreign-made dimestore doodads has, in many cases, left our panels festooned with gyros and aneroids of questionable durability—even U.S.-made equipment is often surprisingly poor in quality control. Airplane owners are forced to resort to instrument R&R (removal and replacement) with increasing frequency. Alas, gyros with 10,000-hour MTBFs (mean time between failures) are apparently a thing of the past—or of the distant future.

Cost-concerned plane owners will therefore want to know something about the removal and replacement of panel instruments. Furthermore, by natural extension, their interest should also embrace the vacuum, pitot-static, and electrical systems. And some dedicated owners may want to update the panel just for the sake of aesthetics and/or efficiency. Panel updating is, of course, a highly personal realm, which we will enter cheerfully. All in good time. First, let's deal with practical matters of damage prevention and control.

WORKING INSIDE THE PANEL

You have a bad tachometer, gyro or other instrument. You've thought the situation over and want to replace the device yourself. It will take work, care, and steady blood pressure, but the result could be well worth the effort. In the next few chapters, we will deal with individual devices, but first there are overall basics and preliminaries to consider.

Required Tools

First, your tool list—which, contrary to what you might think, will have few or no jeweler's specialty items and many common implements that you no doubt already own:

1. A set of small Allen wrenches for loosening knobs from VOR heads, turn-command dials, altimeters, and any other "dialable" instruments that have been poked through the Royalite false panels. If you're fortunate and don't have a custom avionics or instrument installation in your aircraft, these may be optional for your plane. But if mini-Allens are necessary, in order to get the small sizes you need, plan on buying the expanded sets available from a decent auto supplier; seven-piece pocket assortments just won't do. (Be forewarned: the better avionics and instruments use *two* set-screws to retain each knob. Don't just loosen one and then start prying.)

2. An assortment of No. 2 Phillips and blade-type screwdrivers, including a two-inch stubby of each type.

3. A set of nut-drivers, or a 1/4-inch-drive ratchet set with some extensions and a U-joint.

4. A putty knife for prying Royalite false panels loose.

5. Open-end wrenches (not yet metric on airplanes).

6. Portable floodlight or trouble-light.

7. Flashlight.

8. Needle-nose and diagonal pliers, for removing seat rail cotter pins.

9. An asortment of pillows or boat cushions. You're going to spend a bit of time standing on your head, learning why aircraft maintenance technicians are underpaid.

10. Small jars and/or muffin tins to store screws and small parts as they are removed.

11. Safety goggles to protect your eyes from those small parts as they fall in your face.

12. An ohmmeter.

Handling the Seats—with Care

The preliminaries for working on any of the common panel instruments are much the same. You'll almost always want to start by removing the front seats (not to mention any loose debris in the front of the cabin, which should be stored temporarily in the baggage hold). Seats are, of course, commonly secured to seat rails with stops made of aluminum blocks, or with clevis-pinned clips retained by cotter pins. (Some A&Ps have also developed the bad habit of using extra-large cotter pins as stops.) Note the locations, then remove the fore and aft seat stops. Typically, it's most efficient to slide the seats forward until the front legs come off their tracks, then slide the seats aft until the rear legs are free. With practice, you'll be able to do this in one graceful back-and-forth movement.

After taking the seats out, temporarily reinstall the seat stops in their proper holes. Please, *please* do not neglect to put these stops back in when you replace the seats; there is nothing more frightening (or dangerous) than to have the seats slide all the way aft off the rails during takeoff or climb. People have actually died in this kind of accident.

Initial Troubleshooting

Now that you are able to get relatively comfortable on the cabin floor, drag in your cushions and tools and lights, and maybe some radio or recorded entertainment. Before taking anything apart, it is prudent to do some trouble-shooting, figuratively standing on your head with a pillow propped up on the rudder pedals.

Start by making sure that the recalcitrant instrument(s) has a functional power supply, be it electrical, vacuum, or air. For instruments such as EGTs, CHTs, and carb temp gauges, check the integrity and continuity of the wiring with your ohmmeter. It is a good practice to disconnect the leads at both the instrument and its sensor, then check both continuity and the possibility of grounding of the conductor(s). Next, bridge the meter with the ohmmeter probes, lightly brushing the contacts to check the meter's movement (or, in the case of gauges requiring the ship's power, close the circuit in other ways). If the circuit is protected with a fuse or circuit breaker (CB), it makes sense either to bridge the circuit protector or brush the power lead against a ground, to verify and establish continuity.

Satisfied that the meter movement works and that the wiring loom has neither shorts nor breaks, attack the sensor, which is almost always the problem anyway. If you can find the specs for your probe(s), you'll find that they can be immersed in boiling water or hot oil and their resisitance (or thermocouple output) checked with your ohmmeter and a thermometer. Quite commonly, an ohmmeter check will show that the probes have a break in continuity. Service manuals for your aircraft usually describe other troubleshooting techniques.

In the case of vacuum or air-driven gyros, make sure that the vacuum source is functioning by running the engine and checking the vacuum or pneumatic gauge; then record the vacuum reading and ascertain that (above a certain engine speed) it does not vary appreciably with rpm. (An rpm variation might be a clue that the relief valve screen or filter is blocked or dirty.) If the vacuum is available and steady, look for collapsed or bent vacuum lines. On multi-engined aircraft, it is important to develop the habit of starting and shutting down the engines in alternating sequences, as there is a shutttle valve in the system that closes when only one engine is running. Should you have a failed shuttle valve and experience an inflight engine shutdown, you would also lose your vacuum instruments, despite a healthy vacuum pump on the "good" engine. The key point is to note that the instruments actually spool up when you start the left (and on alternate flights, the right) engine alone.

Incidentally, the foregoing procedure is also advisable for checking dual hydraulic pump installations on aircraft so equipped, as most hydraulic systems—even on twins—have only one pressure gauge.

When you are satisfied that you have a regulated and functioning vacuum (or pneumatic) air supply, with lines that are leak-free, uncollapsed, and unobstructed, it's a good idea to change the system filter(s) and clean the vacuum relief valve screen with a dry toothbrush.

Removal Techniques

Let's assume that you have checked all the instrument lines and leads, have surveyed the situation, have exhausted your repertoire of preliminary troubleshooting techniques, and are now insistent about removing an offending instrument.

Most twin-engined aircraft have painted metal panels with each instrument secured by means of three or four flat-head (flush, countersunk) machine screws, or possibly one or two machine screws plus one or two post lights. Lesser aircraft cover their metal instrument panels (again with gauges similarly secured by flat-head or round-head machine screws) with a formed piece of Royalite thermo-plastic. Where this is the case, you can remove the appropriate Royalite false panel (there are usually two or three major segments) by either

Most twins feature flush-mount screws on the instruments, while lots of singles have Royalite panels hiding the instrument screws.

removing the retaining screws around the perimeter and gently prying the panel back with a putty knife, or—when snapped in place—by gently prying the false panel back with the knife, slipping the blade under the snap-in retainers, and popping them. Using your Allen wrenches, remove any avionics or instrument knobs that interfere with false-panel removal. (Look carefully to see whether one or two set-screws are used, before attempting to pry off the knob.) Store knobs carefully, making sure you don't lose any small set-screws.

Typically, the false panel on earlier airplanes was put in place at the factory prior to installation of the control yoke, in which case it now becomes necessary (during maintenance) to tape it out of the way to avoid damage. On later-model Cessnas, however, the false panel has a slot at the bottom so it can be slid over the control column and physically removed. If your plane has post lights, either disconnect the wires or tape them out of the way.

Before removing the instrument retaining screws, it is usually best to uncouple static lines, vacuum lines, cables, or other hookups at the rear of the gauge in question. To do this, you'll probably have to dive under the panel again, although some aircraft have removable glare shields or access panels, or swing-out or pull-out instrument panel bays, which save a lot of grief. (This varies from plane to plane, and even from year to year within airplane model runs.) The gyro instruments are often set in their own shock-mounted quadrant, as well. Stop and look at what you've got.

If you simply cannot get at the instrument's flexible hoses or leads to remove them, it is generally permissible to remove the screws at the front and push the instrument through, letting it hang on the wires or hoses. (Do this as a last resort.) Mark the wires or hoses as they are removed; it will make things much easier at replacement time. (Instruments are commonly removed and sent out for overhaul, which can take several weeks. Unless you have an awesome memory, you can expect that you will forget the specifics.) Don't be like some mechanics and accidentally end up reconnecting the "air in" and "air out" hoses backwards to your DG or artificial horizon.

Normally, instrument attach screws come out easily; however, there may be some surprises. On contemporary airplanes, instrument screws are typically threaded into self-retaining bent-up metal clips call instrument nuts. Older gauges have press-fit nuts on shafts that are superior, but much harder to replace. If your aircraft has had many instruments removed and replaced, it is likely that you'll find that the attach hardware has been bastardized. Typical substitutes are AN310 castle nuts and Tinnerman nut-plates. The latter will invariably drop off and become lost in the circuit breakers at the battery bus. Castle nuts, on the other hand, have such close clearance to the instrument cases that you often cannot use nut-drivers or sockets; you'll have to make do with open-end wrenches. After you fight a castle nut to a draw, it too will fall into the circuit breakers. Retrieve, recover, or otherwise remove these missing nuts. If they do fall into the wiring, they will rattle around like little grenades until they explode (or short out something when you need it most). Then trot off to an avionics shop and get the correct hardware. Instrument nuts come in a universal size and about five dedicated lengths. Don't bother trying to guess; take the instrument with you.

Reassembly Tips

Reassembly is in the reverse order. Make certain the reinstalled hoses or leads do not interfere with any of the aileron or elevator cables; it is easy to twist them around such cables. While standing on your head, with plenty of light, "box" the controls, taking the ailerons and elevator to their stops. Chances are, you did things right—but you may find someone else's work (commonly an avionics wiring loom) interfering with control travel. You'll be amazed, in fact, at what you'll find behind an instrument panel—things that rub, clamps that aren't there, tools, rags, sharp objects, what-have-you. Make certain you recover all hardware. And before you replace the Royalite false panel(s), take a small screwdriver and reset the rate-of-climb (VSI) to zero. It's the small screw in the lower left corner, where you would expect to find another mounting screw. Zero it out, then tap the VSI/ROC case lightly, to see if there is any friction or slack. Adjust it a couple of times, until you are satisfied that your setting is accurate.

In all cases, if you are going to replace an instrument, recall that the regulations require it to have appropriate range markings. For example, don't buy a surplus airspeed indicator from Wag Aero that has Grumman Cougar markings and install it in your Cessna 150. If your IA catches it at annual time, he will have no recourse but to ground the airplane. Gauge markings are found in the appropriate Type Certificate Data Sheets (sometimes in the Pilot's Operating Handbook as well), which your IA is required to have. Several instrument suppliers are listed below. Any of them is equipped to overhaul your instruments and refinish the dials with appropriate range markings; you supply the specs, and they apply them by custom silk-screening.

ICT Instrument, Inc. 1611 S. Eisenhower Wichita, KS 67209	Kelley Instruments, Inc. 1024 Santa Fe Wichita, KS 67211
Air Capital Instruments 1711 S. Knight Suite N Wichita, KS 67277	Midwest Aircraft Instruments, Inc. 4215 W. 220th St. Jordan, MN 55352
Thompson Associates P.O. Box 12032 Wichita, KS 67277	Century Instrument Corp. 4440 Southeast Blvd. Wichita, KS 67210

Protection from Heat Strokes

When it comes to extending the MTBF of instruments and avionics, experience has proven that it pays to protect your instrument panel with canopy covers or thermal screens any time you park your plane outside in warm-weather. At the very least, draping a space blanket (L.L. Bean or equivalent) over the panel yields rewards far exceeding the $10 initial investment. Airplanes with light-colored panels—late-model Beeches and Cessnas—tend to fare far better than Pipers and others having funereal black (solar-absorbing) panels. The reason, of course, is that cabin tempreatures can easily shoot past levels at which lubricants (not to mention compass fluid) evaporate and O-rings dry out and leak. (While the Dow Corning grease used on gyro pivots is fairly tenacious, there are viscous dampers in many turn-and-banks which can actually leak fluid under adverse conditions.) Such leaks, when present in the static system, can be profoundly important and may require expensive overhauls. Usually, you'll learn about them when you present your aircraft for its biennial pitot-static check, which is mandatory for IFR flight.

THE MAGNETIC COMPASS

Some airplanes carry the magnetic compass within the panel; most of today's general aviation airplanes do not. In either case, it is important not to overlook this crucial instrument or take it for granted, for however much gyro and electronic navigation equipment we may load into our panels, the wet magnetic compass's message is like home plate in orienting the navigational ballpark. And, as many pilots learn each year, when the more sophisticated equipment suddenly becomes unreliable or nonfunctional—especially in IFR—the magnetic compass had better be faithfully on the job or chaos may ensue.

Let's deviate briefly for a look into maintaining the magnetic compass, even though it may not be part of your instrument panel.

Compass Vulnerabilities

In terms of overall simplicity and reliability, the magnetic compass is surely one of the most foolproof devices in a modern cockpit (never mind the fact that it's also one of the most ancient). What, you might well wonder, could possibly go wrong with a simple magnet floating in kerosene (or alcohol, or whatever)?

For one thing, summer heat has a way of making wet compasses go dry, and when compasses go dry (or malfunction for any reason whatever), you're grounded, technically speaking. Federal Aviation Regulation 91.33(b) requires every standard-category U.S. aircraft to have a functioning "magnetic direction indicator" for VFR flight. (Oddly, there are no regulations governing the degree of accuracy of the compass system; you simply must have one, accurate or not.)

There are other ills to consider, as well. Excessive card oscillation

The filler plug on this Airpath C2300 compass allows the operator to service the instrument with MIL-C-5020A compass fluid in the field, without removal of the instrument from the aircraft.

can occur when air bubbles form in the top of the instrument case, allowing the fluid to slosh across the top of the card. A sluggish card can result from pivot damage, weak magnets, or—more commonly—excessive compensation (which itself may have been invited by improper installation of avionics or other equipment that might be interfering with the compass).

And then there's the most common trouble of all—excessive card error (i.e., inaccurate indications).

The possible causes are legion: Perhaps you installed a new cockpit speaker, but paid no attention to speaker-magnet weight. Or maybe you simply moved your existing speaker from one location in the cockpit to another. Maybe a maintenance technician installed a new instrument using steel (rather than brass or aluminum) hardware. Or you've brought portable electronic equipment into the cockpit environment. Or you installed new seat belts, and one of the latches is magnetized. Or you had one of your seats repaired by heli-arc welding, and the seat structure itself is now polarized. Any of these or a hundred other things could cause your compass to indicate incorrectly, necessitating a reswinging. (By the way, when *was* the last time you had your compass swung?)

We don't advocate, by the way, that you swing your compass yourself—or do any other compass maintenance unaided. From a legal standpoint, neither you nor your A&P may do any of the things that a compass manufacturer would call "maintenance." (FAR 65.81 prohibits A&Ps from making "any repair to, or alteration of, instruments.") *The pointers offered in this article are for educational purposes only. What you do with the information is up to you—and your instrument repairman.*

Fluid Replenishment

Although wet compasses come from the factory well sealed, it is possible for fluid to be lost due to evaporation over a long time. When this happens, air bubbles can form in the top of the chamber, leading to a variety of ills, chief among them improper dampening of the card. (The spinning portion of the compass is properly called the "card".) Air entering the system can damage the card's upper pivot bearing and also can begin oxidation of the compass fluid, clouding it.

Servicing a compass with fluid *is*, in our opinion, something you *can* legally do yourself, if your compass is of the field-fillable Airpath C2300 kind. (The over-whelming majority of wet compasses used in piston-engine general aviation aircraft are of the panel-mount, pedestal-mount, or overhead-mount 2-1/4-inch type, made by Airpath Instrument Co., St. Louis, MO 63155.) If you have access to a filler plug, you can simply remove the plug and top the instrument off with an eyedropper or syringe full of compass fluid. (Most wet compasses now use kerosene or aliphatic naphtha rather than alcohol, but smell yours anyway, just to be sure.)

Another, better way to fill your compass is to remove it from the panel, empty all the old fluid, and fill the unit up by submerging it in a pail of fresh compass fluid, rocking it gently to dispel trapped bubbles. (Before you do this, tape off the opening to the compensating-magnet chamber. This chamber is intended to remain dry.) Close off the case before withdrawing the instrument from the fluid.

Note: Don't worry about accidentally knocking the card off its gimbals—Airpath compasses are "non-tumbling," even if they become inverted. Also, don't worry about having to reswing the compass after refilling it with fluid. As long as you did not make any other adjustments to it, it should read the same after you install it. (*Do*

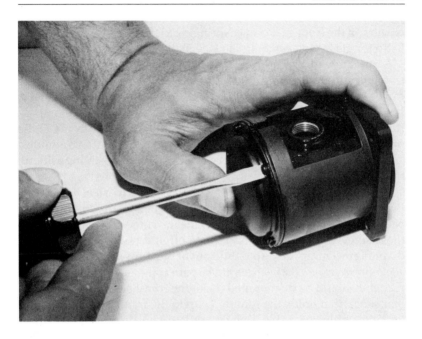

After unscrewing and removing the back-plate, you can lift off the elastic diaphragm, as shown here. (Metal plate underneath is part of the instrument case and is intended to protect internal mechanisms.)

remember to save and reuse those mounting screws: They're non-magnetic brass.)

Diaphragm Replacement

Evaporation loss is one thing, but catastrophic loss of fluid is another. If your compass has gone dry completely, or is dripping fluid (either of which will leave your cockpit smelling like JP-4), chances are good the instrument has a dried out, ripped, or otherwise defective diaphragm.

If you've ever taken an aircraft compass apart, you will have noticed that at the rear of the instrument case, sandwiched between the case and the rear end-plate, is a flexible gasket or diaphragm that covers the entire rear of the compass. The purpose of this diaphragm, of course, is to [1] seal the case off in leak-free fashion, and [2] provide a relief mechanism for the thermal expansion of fluid that takes place when a compass is exposed to a 200° cockpit on a summer day. (There is a gasket at the front, too, to seal the glass at the instrument's face, but the chances of the front gasket ever springing a leak are extremely remote. Ditto for glass replacement: The face plate is quite thick.)

Fortunately, diaphragm replacement is neither tricky nor expensive nor time-consuming. New diaphragms (Airpath P/N C21-100) can be had for but a few dollars from Candle Aviation Supply (1640A Lincoln Avenue, Holbrook NY 11740), and MIL-C-5020A compass fluid is similarly inexpensive by the quart and obtainable from Candle or almost any large FBO. Replacement should take about five minutes.

Start by dismounting the compass from the aircraft, setting aside all the mounting screws where they won't get lost. (Remember, these are special non-steel screws that *must not be replaced* with steel hardware.) Putting the compass face down on a work bench, unscrew the four back-plate screws on the rear end of the instrument case (again, save those screws); then lift the back-plate off and remove the ruptured diaphragm. Dump all the old fluid out of the compass. *Be careful not to allow dirt to get into the instrument.* Airpath compasses with a rounded rear end should be dismounted (from the front) before removing the rear screw that holds the rounded cup to the frame. That rear screw isn't generally reachable anyway, unless you dismount the whole compass first. The rounded cup pulls off to reveal a standard Airpath frame with filler plug at the top and diaphragm hold-down plate at the rear.

After soaking your new diaphragm in MIL-C-5020A compass fluid, fill the instrument case with fluid (you can postpone this step if there's a filler plug elsewhere on the case), lay the diaphragm in its proper place on the rear of the compass, and put the back-plate on, tightening all the screws until snug. (Take care not to strip the soft-metal screws.) As mentioned before, the best way to fill the instrument is to submerge it in fluid and tap it to dispel bubbles—but again, first seal off the compensating-magnet chamber with tape. (The chamber should remain dry throughout.) When you're done, reinstall the compass exactly where it was before, using exactly the same screws that were used before. Be sure not to introduce steel screws to the compass environment. If you lose a brass screw, find an identical brass replacement. A further note of caution: Don't mistake compensation screws for installation hardware; the installation screws are invariably outboard of the compensation screws, and all are brass, that is, nonmagnetic. Finally, do *not* repaint the compass unless you are sure that the paint you are using has no metallic pigments.

Then, at last but not least, be sure to get your repairman to sign off

the work in your airframe log, if you want to remain legal. In addition, be sure to tell your A&P that under FAR 43.3(d)—the "supervision" regs—he, too, can replace compass diaphragms legally ... with a repairman's signoff.

REFASHIONING THE PANEL

To get at the thermal-relief diaphragm, all you have to do is unscrew the brass or aluminum retaining screws holding the back-plate to the instrument body. (Don't lose those screws or try to substitute steel ones later; only nonmagnetic hardware is acceptable in a compass.)

We turn now from the mundane to what can be grandly sublime: refashioning the panel according to one's own vision of what makes for good gauge efficiency or is just good looking. Panel updating is a fascinating field on which are strewn results ranging from magnificent successes to head-pounding failures, as owners have sought to reflect shifts in fashion, accommodate to technology's new opportunities, and escape mass-marketing mediocrity.

For some pilots, such work amounts to a proud cause.

Time Warpage

Except for the fact that older airplanes seem to have been built with better materials and craftsmanship, little of substance separates a 1965 Cessna 182 from the latest model Skylane. What's true of Skylanes holds also for many other aircraft, including such diverse types as Barons and Bellanca Vikings. Most light aircraft that are still in production trace their lineage directly to designs of the 1940s and 50s; the latest versions vary only in detail design.

But detail design is very important. Your impression of what makes a modern plane "modern" is tied directly to such mundane matters as door latches, escutcheons, and seat padding, which have undergone steady improvement over a period of decades. Postwar airplanes up through the early sixties show their age most vividly in their dated panel designs. Fortunately, most instrument panels can be dramatically updated, if you've got the time and money—or at least, the time and willingness to do a lot of the work yourself.

The motivation for updating instrument panels isn't limited to aesthetics; on many airplanes, there is a need to replace antique AN-type gyroscopic instruments with later, smaller designs. There's always the need to find adequate instrument panel space for more avionics, too, although contemporary avionics are making life much easier in this respect.

And then there's the matter of ergonomics (the science of making controls and machines "user-friendly" for maximum effectiveness and safety). The classic example of poor ergonomics, of course, is Beech's long unchanging placement of the Bonanza's flap selector switch where everyone else puts the gear switch. (On the other hand, Beech's Sundowner, Sierra, and Duchess series have exceptionally cleanly designed panels. Maybe it's just that Beech doesn't believe in redesigning anything until it has clearly been defeated by the test of time.)

Where Beech was content to leave its instrument panels alone for decades at a time, Cessna has tended to change its panel layouts with predictable regularity. That's not to say that Cessna hasn't been at the forefront of making panel designs user-friendly. We marvel, in fact, at the openness and apparent simplicity of the instrument panels of all of Cessna's newer multiengine airplanes, up to and including the Citations. Everything seems to be in just the right place, with no big surprises (which is not something you can say after a panel tour of a Swearingen or an early Lear, much less such monstrosities as a Beech Super 18 panel). And the Cessna singles? The panel on a 1977 Cessna 180 is a model of simplicity compared to that of generations of Bellancas and Mooneys, not to mention the funereal black panels of early Piper singles.

With that in mind, to update the panel layout of virtually any Cessna, one might merely go to the parts book or savage yard and pick up the appropriate pieces for the latest model of the series in question. Yet would anyone actually go to the trouble of updating a 1965 Skylane panel to a 1984 configuration? The original design is not bad, varying degrees of success. Most are done to get contemporary

Factory placards were peeling off author's panel before rework.

placement of flight instruments and center-stacking of avionics. Most mount the instruments on 0.125-inch 2024-T3 or 6061-T6 aluminum plate stock, then hang that subpanel on existing shock mountings.

If the pedestrian Cessnas rarely get total panel updates, it may be because their owners are a bit more pragmatic than the owners of cult airplanes. It may also be because such prosaic aircraft have been pretty much relegated to VFR use only, unlike early Bonanzas, Comanches, and Mooneys. The latter planes, though quite old in some cases, still appeal for IFR use (and of course remain fine transportation today). Owners of such aircraft seem to have recognized that their utility in the modern ATC environment can be dramatically up-graded with careful panel up-dating. The marketplace has responded accordingly.

The Piper Comanche's panel—in contrast to the lavish Beech panels of identical vintage—is of simple sheetmetal construction and is much easier to update. Ray Frey (Five Grand Court, San Rafael, CA 94901) sells panel drawings, instructions, and a Xerox copy of the Form 337 used on his airplane. As with the original design, panels built to Frey's configuration are shock-mounted; the current philosophy, by contrast, seems to be that the hard mounting of instrument panels is satisfactory, given today's Dynafocal engine mounts. As a nice touch,

Frey had his own panel brush-finished and black-anodized. (Note: He does not sell parts—only drawings and information.)

Dennis Ashby (135 Lido Way, Upland, CA 91786) markets a fiberglass glareshield for single and Twin Comanches with a leather texture and black semi-gloss color for $150, with optional lights built in for an addition $30. He claims that the glareshield can be installed without removing the windshield. Combining Frey's panel with Ashby's glareshield and then relettering the subpanel should bring an old Comanche right up into the '80s (particularly if you splurge for a one-piece windshield to boot).

Early Mooney panels have long seemed the ultimate in tack and sleaze, complementing their miserly radio stack space. Some panel updates are available through Miller Air Sports, Rt. 2 Box 356D, San Marcos, TX 78666, the same people who market a host of 201-style cowl and windshield changes. Owner Jon Svendsen removed the old panel of his 1966 Super 21 and rebuilt it, finding room to add not only the usual dual navcoms, DME, and transponder, but dual ADFs (for trans-Atlantic flights). He also built a glareshield of vinyl-covered balsa. Other than purchasing a new stack of avionics, this panel update was remarkably inexpensive, at $100 or so for materials. As with any panel modifications, it was excruciatingly labor-intensive (Svendsen built three panels before he was satisfied). The end result was exemplary; Mooney should have done as well. Svendsen also painted the new panel with Piper instrument-panel white, as used on late Aztecs and Navajos. It looks right.

The range of possibilities is limited only by your imagination and free time. Of course, on any potential project of this sort, your first step should be to join the Marque club associated with your particular plane (the list is quite long; consult the latest AOPA Handbook for Pilots under "Addresses and Services, Aviation Organizations," or call AOPA at 301/695-2000) and review others' efforts. Happily, panel modifying is not particularly expensive if you do the work yourself. About all you need to purchase is some sheet metal, miscellaneous hardware, bulb angles, and shock mounts. Unfortunately, the design differences among aircraft models (even in various years of the same model line) are so numerous that it doesn't make sense to go into detail on any one model here, but we can advise you on a few things:

First, before you start, review your objectives with a sympathetic IA (Inspection Authorization holder). Anticipate the need for an FAA field approval of the paperwork. Anything you do beyond refinishing

Ray Frey's modified Comanche panel. Note single-piece windshield, Aztec control yokes, neat avionics stack.

will constitute a major alteration that must be recorded on a Form 337. At that, your IA cannot by himself return your aircraft to service, but will need the FAA's assistance (which is the essence of a field approval) and physical inspection of the completed project. Some airplanes, such as the Navion, have instrument panels that are part of the primary structure of the airplane and cannot readily be modified. This sort of thing is the prime reason for first visiting your IA. Don't cut metal until such problems have been addressed.

Once the basic feasibility is established, consider reviewing your objectives with your accountant and spouse. While modernizing a panel can be emotionally rewarding, with the current bloodbath in the marketplace it may be worth absorbing a loss on your present aircraft in order to update a decade or so. Sometimes a change of airplanes is the best way to go. Why try to turn a C35 Bonanza into an ersatz S35, if you can buy the S35 for the same money? The C35 is a good airplane, but the difference is that with the older plane you're fighting a constant uphill battle against availability of prop parts, generators, solenoids, and other bits and pieces that can only continue to become more and more restrictive for old complex airplanes.

Confine your efforts to changing the layouts of avionics and instruments, then making cosmetic improvements to control and switch panels. Modifying subpanels requires super-motivation; one rule modifiers soon learn is that when you change or relocate one item, you invariably end up needing to change three or four more downstream. Svendsen's subpanel incorporates all original controls and switches and has mostly cosmetic changes. The same is true of Frey's Comanche panel and most of Beryl D'Shannon's Baron and Bonanza mods. Subpanels generally respond very well to disassembly, repainting, and relettering.

If you're moving avionics from a lower or side panel location to do a center-stack upgrade, anticipate the need for a new wiring harness and new antenna leads. Your first priority should be to make a dimensional check of the planned space behind the panel. To do a total Frey-style update on an old Comanche can mean replacing several antennas to extend their leads, plus splicing or otherwise redoing much of the avionics wiring harness, and stepping up the size of the pitot-static line.

Once you're committed, disconnect the battery to preclude any chance of shorting out a power bus. Remove the old panel and instruments, tagging everything. If you can do it, remove the panel as an assembly—it may then be possible to trace around it, using it as a pattern for the new panel, then reinstall the old panel to eliminate aircraft downtime while experimenting with mockups and layout

Jon Svendsen's 1966 Mooney Super 21 panel, after redesign. Note that the T-configuration gauges are outlined with black striping tape. Post lights were added during redesign.

The labels shown here were done with Presstype.

designs. Hope that you can use the original shock-mounting hard-ware or hard attach points; these should be scribed, drilled, or other-wise defined on your pattern at this time. The pattern should be of dimensionally stable material, such as light-gauge metal or inexpen-sive fiberglass or plastic sheet.

After removing the old panel, tape over any static source ports and gyro inlets/outlets, and tape over the ends of static and vacuum lines. Label each and every wire, hose, and line. If your aircraft does not have an alternate static source or a remote vacuum filter, now is the time to incorporate these worthwhile additions. (Also, if your windshield needs replacing, *do it now*. And don't get a pitot-static system check the week before starting this project, because a new check will be required after you complete your modifications. A static check is required whenever a static instrument, line, or fixture is disturbed.

Inspect the existing mounting fixtures and locations. Again, if at all possible, use those mounting points in your redesign. A statement on your Form 337 to the effect that "existing primary instrument panel structure and shock mountings were left intact" goes a long way with the FAA when your request for field approval is considered.

Eliminating shock mounts can result in setting the panel back far enough that necessary instrument and avionics clearance is lost. A quarter inch can ruin you. Carefully check for obstacles such as steel tubing or aluminum structure, battery boxes, and control yoke fixtures and cables which will restrict the layout on your new design. The space behind the panel is invariably filled with spaghetti.

If you are going to add anything, such as a vernier control for the mixture, check before enlarging the existing hole. On the Comanche, a lot of room has to be left around the control yoke shaft for its moving fixtures and hardware; this means the large original gyro instruments cannot be located directly above the yoke in the classic 'T' configuration—a problem rectified by using new 3-1/8-inch instruments. Other aircraft have similar constraints.

It is common to make the new panel slightly larger than the original, if the original metal or Royalite fascia is to be discarded. In such cases, be sure to allow for settling of the panel in its shock mounts. When you hang 40 pounds or so of instruments and avionics on a single sheet and allow for 6-*g* loading, it is possible to run into unanticipated control interference. (Even if you never fly aerobatics, you can get 6-*g* loading by taxiing across a pothole.)

Remember also that fluid lines should not be located above electrical wiring. On non-transport-category aircraft, it is possible to have primers with fuel lines in the cockpit, as well as oil-filled oil-pressure-gauge lines, fluid-filled fuel-pressure lines, etc. (to say nothing of hydraulic lines to gauges, switches, and/or power packs).

Also remember that even the latest solid-state panel-mount avionics demand adequate cooling. The most effective manner of providing ventilation appears to be simply elevating the glare shield a quarter inch or so above the panel structure. (What's good enough for a King Air is good enough for you.)

Black hardware seems to be the most desirable aesthetically. You can find black panel screws at any avionics shop or via the big catalog houses. Don't substitute steel screws for brass screws, however (your compass won't like it). Where steel is permissible, you can save money by buying ordinary machine screws and bluing them with gun blue (see your sporting goods store). Flush screws are most attractive, but it is very difficult to make an entire panel without misdrilling, and round-head screws allow you to cover up minor mistakes.

Whatever type of screws you use, get an instrument layout mask (from Aircraft Spruce and Specialty, Box 424, Fullerton, CA 92632, or from any of the big catalog shops found in *Trade-A-Plane* for layout of the instrument holes. Remember that the instruments' cases are larger than their 2.25-inch and 3.125-inch faces; measure and allow appropri-

Letters are waterproofed via clear-lacquer topcoat.

ate clearances. Good old 6061-T6 aluminum is the most common alloy for panels, and in eighth-inch thickness a band saw is the most effective means of cutting, with edges then filed smooth and corners radiused. Anywhere it is necessary to use an inside corner, the corner should first be laid out and drilled with a bit of about 3/16 or 1/4-inch and then cut to that hole.

Instrument holes can be cut with a precision fly cutter in a vertical mill or drill press, if the work is securely clamped in place. Center-drill each location with a 1/16-inch drill and then take the panel in to an avionics shop for punching.

Avionics stacks can be built as a one-piece panel via 1/2 x 1 x 1/16 inch extruded angle brackets flush-riveted or bolted into place for attachment of the radio cans. Better than that, though, may be to use two or three separate pieces for the panel, which will make maintenance much easier, then building up the radio racks in such a manner that they attach the main panel structure. In any case, try to allow some vertical clearance (1/4-inch, say) between radios for adequate cooling.

After you've done your paper layouts and mockups and you've finished cutting metal for the final panels, sand out any scratches or tooling marks with 320-grit paper. Make sure you scuff the entire panel before painting. Using a primer is not of any great advantage, unless it is an epoxy type that has greater tenacity—they all seem to chip with equal frequency, in my experience. Flat black looks fine in Royalite and in military airplanes, but it tends to look cheap when applied to panels in general aviation airplanes (and has no proven virtues such as being easy on the eyes). Use what you want, though.

After painting the panel, do any lettering before installing the instruments. It is easiest to do all lettering with the panel flat on the kitchen table or workbench—you'll blow it if you wait until the panel is in the airplane. Pitot lines, vacuum hoses, and other hookups can be lengthened at this time to allow the main panel to be fully assembled before installation, making later service and maintenance much easier. If you folow this suggestion, though, make sure the surplus wiring and hoses cannot interfere with controls after the panel is reinstalled. When splicing wires and such, make certain you purchase aircraft-quality materials (at an avionics shop); automotive stuff won't do.

As you can see, panel modifications allow you tremendous design latitude—unlike virtually any other changes you wish to make on an airplane. Give your creative bent free rein. Chances are good you'll make it better than most factory efforts—right about the time you finish your third mockup and redesign.

Sweating the Details

Panel modification and artistry converge most individualistically and with particular intensity when owners take extra steps to enhance the panel's outward appearance. There are various ways of approaching such work, of course, and no single strategy is definitive, but there are techniques and resources that anyone attempting it should constantly keep in mind.

The experience of *LPM* contributing editor Michael L. Stockhill in detailing the panel of his venerable Piper Comanche is highly instructive as a guide. Stockhill describes his labors, problems, and solutions as follows:

When dealing with instrument panel modifications, the difference between a mess and a masterpiece is craftsmanship—attention to detail. While matters such as color choice and texture are up for grabs (who's to say whether battleship grey, flat black, or inlaid walnut is better?), the manner in which placards and circuit-breaker labels are detailed out can make or break an otherwise acceptable panel facelift.

The factories use several techniques for labeling. Cessna embosses the Royalite false panels on its single-engined line; Beech relies heavily

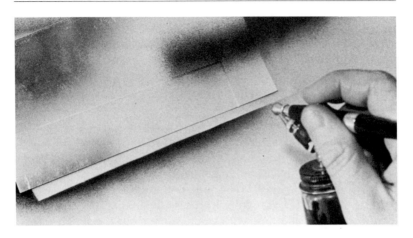

Black coat is airbrushed on over the trimline tape and white coat.

on decals; and Piper is notorious for using adhesive-backed aluminum labels (in what seems to be an overwhelming abundance) that start peeling off the day they leave the factory. Radio shops often use small placards of engraved plastic; many A&Ps use Dymo labels (which I find particularly nasty) to relabel various switches. And finally, a number of aircraft have their placards and labels painted on metal subpanels.

If you really want to get elaborate, you can countersink all instruments and switches in a piece of coated Plexiglas that is then engraved and backlit with grain-of-wheat bulbs. This type of panel or subpanel has been common for years in Aero Commanders and many custom avionics installations in corporate aircraft. The technique seems to have fallen into disfavor in recent years, however, possibly because it is so labor-intensive. However, it was used to advantage by Bruce Whittig on his 1983 EAA award-winning Midget Mustang.

When I restored my old Comanche, I knew that it would be imperative to remove the painted green subpanel and repaint the instrument panel, for my color choice for the rest of the interior was a deep red. Not wishing to make a mess of the job, I spent a lot of time selecting the best means to relabel all the switches, controls, and circuit breakers.

My first attempt was to purchase a set of panel decals (available in black or white for $6.75 from Sky Sales, 11548 Louise Ave., Granada Hills, CA 91344). Each package has over 1,400 words and numerals, on a thin sheet of transparent plastic self-stick adhesive. To use this system, each word, letter, or number is cut out with scissors or a razor blade and then stuck in place, much as you would do with a piece of Mystic tape (or even a ... shudder ... Dymo label). It didn't take me long to realize that use of the Sky Sales labels simply wouldn't meet my standards, although I'd find them satisfactory for labeling the occasional odd switch or control.

I knew there had to be a better way. My friend Jon Svendsen, who did such an elaborate reengineering of his Mooney Super 21's panel, suggested using Presstype (letters that are transferred from their wax-paper substrate to the underlying suface by pressure from the opposite side of the wax paper), as he had done, and then fixing the letters with clear lacquer. I viewed the process of spelling out individual words one letter at a time with trepidation, since the slightest misalignment would be clearly evident.

Not long after hearing his suggestion, I ran across similar dry trasfer labels that spell out common instrument panel words in an Aircraft Spruce & Specialty catalog. The labels were available in both black and white, in two sizes (10-pt. and 12-pt.), for a bit less than the Sky Sales panel labels. I was sold.

If you need only to use a word or two for labels on an existing panel, just clean the area with soap and water, followed by a mild solvent such as Prep-Sol, then rub on the appropriate label, and you're on your way. If durability is a consideration, fix the label with a light overcoat of clear lacquer. Should you be building up a new panel or refinishing an old subpanel, your preparations must obviously be a bit more elaborate.

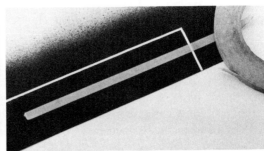

At left, trim tape can now be peeled off. Note that the paint should have been thinned for more consistent flow (although it is possible to deliberately obtain the textured finish shown. At right, a thicker width of thinline tape can be used as a guide line for dry transfer lettering.

Rubbing with a dull pencil causes dry transfer labels (on the underside of the plastic sheet) to transfer to the panel. For best results, make many soft strokes, not several hard strokes, of the pencil.

I stripped my Comanche's subpanel to bare metal after very carefully diagramming and labeling the switch and circuit breaker names and locations on a piece of drawing paper. I then polished the surface with 320- and 400-grit wet-or-dry abrasive paper, which leaves enough tooth for paint to stick. Next, I primed it with some zinc chromate aerosol, followed by a color coat sprayed on with an airbrush (available from most model airplane supply stores). For my finish coat, I bought a pint of Gulfstream Commander instrument panel grey for $32; I've since concluded that a couple of $1.50 bottles of model railroad paints would have worked just as satisfactorily. (Such paints are available in a myriad of colors to satisfy any palate—

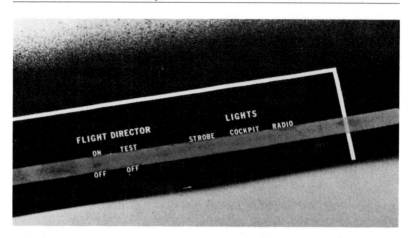

The above photo shows labels in place, before removal of the masking-tape guide. After removing the guide tape, letters can be fixed by overcoating with clear lacquer.

or any palette.) For the instrument panel itself, I elected to use 400-grit paper to scuff the original paint surface, after first cleaning it with soap and water and Prep-Sol. Then I masked it carefully and shot a coat of automotive sandable primer, available in aerosol, before using the airbrush to apply the color coat.

Since I wanted to duplicate the fine lines used on the original panel, I carefully masked off the lines I wanted with quarter-inch masking tape (one of many various widths of a special fine-edge Scotch brand tape quite unlike ordinary masking tape). This tape, available from Aircraft Spruce & Specialty, is a pastel zinc-chromate color, and is also found at automotive paint shops.

Once I was satisfied that the lines were straight and true, I masked off the balance of the panel with pieces of newspaper and ordinary masking tape.

Again, I shot the white lines with the airbrush, using model railroad paints. How silly of me—I later realized that I could have sprayed white first, laid fine-line trim tape (from the model shop) as a masking tape, shot the final colors over that tape, and removed it, leaving clean, neat, even white lines.

The same sequence could also have been used for dark lines on a light background by shooting on a coat of dark paint before masking (understanding that it is harder to cover dark paint with lighter colors). If you wish, it's acceptable to just lay out the final lines with the fine-line trim tapes—which are available in several colors—and fix them with clearcoat (which is what Jon Svendsen did on his Mooney).

Once the final panel paint dried, I used the masking tape to define and align the Presstype label sites, carefully measuring them and their projected locations for centering and providing appropriate guidelines. The Presstype was then transferred, using a blunt soft pencil tip or an old ballpoint as a burnishing tool to rub the letters off the wax paper. The process is easier done than described. *[Hint: Make a lot of soft strokes with the burnishing tool, not two or three strokes of heavy pressure per letter—Ed.]*

Once all the labels are in place, remove the masking tape guides, then cover the labels with a coat of artist's matte spray or flat clearcoat (available in aerosol or in bottles, from the model supply shop).

When we do the actual work of flying—especially instrument flying—the organization and beauty of the panel pales in importance beside the ability of the panel to tell us the truth. To keep them honest calls for understanding and protecting *their* sources of information. That is the subject of the following chapters.

Chapter 2

VACUUM AND PITOT-STATIC SYSTEM MAINTENANCE

The accuracy of our heading, attitude, and altitude instruments depends upon the integrity of the systems that feed them. Protecting the directional gyro, artificial horizon (attitude indicator), altimeter, and vertical speed indicator rests heavily on proper maintenance of the vacuum and pitot-static systems. The measures owner-pilots can take range from observations made during regular preflight walk-arounds and runups through digging into hidden mechanisms that are often neglected because we do not understand how these systems can fail. This chapter is intended to provide some useful education along those lines.

VACUUM SYSTEMS AND THEIR PROBLEMS

Vacuum systems (as used to power non-electric gyro instruments) need maintenance from time to time and *will* break down if neglected. Pilots who know how to perform this maintenance are in a position to double or triple gyro instrument life (and save some money at annual-inspection time, too). Pilots who *don't* know how to do this work are wasting money (and/or instrument life) needlessly.

Vacuum Systems

Before we get into the actual "here's how" of vacuum system maintenance, let's take a moment to review some basics of vacuum system operation and design.

Suction to operate such intruments as the DG and artificial horizon comes either from a gear-driven *vacuum pump* mounted on the engine accesssory case or (in the case of older aircraft) a fuselage-mounted *venturi*. To control system pressure, an adjustable screening device known as a *suction relief valve* is placed between the pump and the instruments, usually on the cockpit side of the firewall.

In older aircraft, the suction lines leading from the relief valve terminate at the instruments themselves; to keep the gauges from becoming contaminated with dust, individual filter elements are installed in each instrument. In most newer aircraft—including all post-1965 single-engine Cessnas—suction tubing runs from the relief valve to the gyro instruments to a *suction gauge*, and thence to a *central air filter* (mounted underneath the panel). Air is thus evacuated first through the main filter, then through the suction gauge, and then through the gyro instruments.

It should be noted that even in aircraft having a central filter system, *individual filters are still used in the gyro instruments themselves.*

Pumps: Wet vs. Dry

All vacuum pumps are sliding-vane type pumps; however, the method of lubrication varies from unit to unit. Some airplanes (certain single-engine Cessnas and Bonanzas, for example) have "wet" pumps, while others (Piper Cherokees and Mooneys, to name just a couple) come with "dry" pumps.

A wet-type pump sucks engine oil through a special Garlock seal to lubricate its vanes. The pump's discharge is through a device known as an *air-oil separator*, which (as you might guess) separates the oil and air coming from the pump so that the former can be returned to the engine and the latter can be expelled overboard. If you have one of these devices, you'll be able to spot it easily; look for a round, black can with three hoses leading to it at the rear of your engine.

Dry-type pumps do not require an air-oil separator. The sliding vanes contained in these units are of the self-lubricating Teflon or Nylon kind. (We will discuss dry pumps in detail shortly.)

Air-Oil Separator Maintenance

Air-Oil separators should be periodically cleaned by washing in Stoddard solvent and drying with compressed air. (Ask your mechanic to show you how to do this, if it's not one of the procedures included in your shop's "flat-rate" annual-inspection fee.) If separators are not kept clean, they clog up—and engine oil will come over in the vacuum pump air-discharge line, coating the bottom of the plane with oil. Any plane that either has a thoroughly grimy belly or seems to be going through oil at a rapid rate should be checked for a

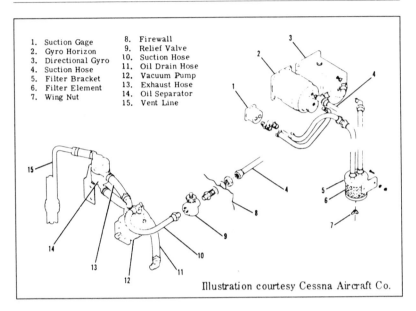

1. Suction Gage
2. Gyro Horizon
3. Directional Gyro
4. Suction Hose
5. Filter Bracket
6. Filter Element
7. Wing Nut
8. Firewall
9. Relief Valve
10. Suction Hose
11. Oil Drain Hose
12. Vacuum Pump
13. Exhaust Hose
14. Oil Separator
15. Vent Line

Illustration courtesy Cessna Aircraft Co.

Basic components of the vacuum system in a typical Cessna single.

clogged air-oil separator. To do this, first determine which of the vent lines that exit the bottom of your plane's cowling is the air-oil separator vent line; then see if you can trace the oil streak(s) on the plane's belly to this line. If you can, you've got a clogged separator.

If—on the other hand—you find that the belly oil is traceable to the *crankcase* vent line(s), you may need a top overhaul since a badly streaking breather line can be an indication of excessive blow-by from the compression chambers. (It could also mean you're overfilling the engine with oil, so don't panic).

Filter Replacement

Any type of filter element will (if it does its job) eventually clog up and need to be replaced or cleaned. This is true of vacuum-system air filters, too.

Cessna, Mooney, and most other airframe manufacturers recommend replacement of individual instrument filter elements *every 100 hours* or whenever erratic or sluggish gyro responses are evident when normal suction-gauge readings are observed, for those aircraft that *do not* have a central air filtration system. For planes that *do* have a central air filtration setup, the usual recommendation is that the main air filter be changed *every 500 hours* (or more often, if conditions warrant) and the instrument filters replaced upon overhaul of the instruments. (If your FBO is charging you for replacement of the main vacuum filter at every annual and you fly only 100 hours a year, you're being taken advantage of. From now on, reach under the panel and change the central vacuum filter yourself every 500 hours— and tell your shop personnel to keep their hands off.) Vacuum air filters (gauge and system type) can be ordered from airframe manufacturers through their dealer networks. Both types of filter element are inexpensive (the "system" type is the more costly of the two), and installation is disarmingly simple. (More about that later in this chapter.)

Because the internal workings of gyroscopic instruments are so delicate, it is very important that vacuum filters be replaced promptly at the times indicated, especially if the aircraft is being operated in a dusty environment and *especially* if cigarette smoke is allowed to enter the cockpit. After all, the air that drives vacuum-driven instruments is drawn *from the aircraft cockpit*. If you or your passengers smoke, that smoke (with its tars and nicotine) goes first through the system filters, then through the gauges themselves.

In case you think this is not a serious matter, consider these comments from a well-known A&P of 30-plus years' experience: "I can look at the outside of a DC-4 and tell you if it used to carry freight of passengers, for in the passenger aircraft, the fuselage rivets will have tiny brown stains streaking downwind, where the lower outside ambient pressure has sucked nicotine out of the interior of the aircraft and caused it to weep by the rivets."

Keep Those Gyros Warm

If you want your vacuum-powered instruments to lead a long, happy life and give you true and accurate readings at all times, be sure

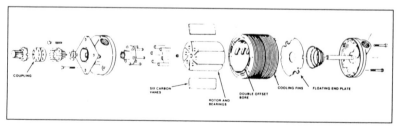

Components of the typical dry vacuum pump (Airborne).

This is the top side of the PA-24 vacuum relief valve or regulator.

your cabin heater works in the winter. Most pilots don't know it (and most operating manuals never mention it), but there's a good reason why *cabin* air—rather than outside air—is used to power vacuum instruments: Namely, the minimum cockpit temperature allowable when suction instruments are installed is 40°F. Many air-powered gauges will not function properly below this temperature. (Bear this in mind if you find yourself without a heater on an IFR flight.)

Suction Gauge Indications

Aside from replacing filter elements on a regular basis and keeping the cockpit air reasonably warm in flight, probably the single most important vacuum-system preventive maintenance measure a pilot can take is to keep careful track of suction-gauge indications.

On most aircraft equipped with an engine-driven vacuum pump, a suction gauge reading of 5.3 inches Hg (inches of mercury) at 1,900 rpm is optimal, with anything between 4.6 and 5.4 inches being acceptable. (For venturi-equipped aircraft, the reading—at cruise speed—will be in the 3.5- to 5.4-inch range.) If you're not seeing 5.3 inches at an egine speed of 1,900 rpm (for Mooneys: 4.7 inches at 1700 rpm), adjust your vacuum relief valve to give the proper indication.

(Note: Do not adjust the relief valve with the engine running. Perform all adjustments in accordance with the manufacturer's recommendations.)

Should you find that you are unable to obtain more than a few inches of suction, no matter how the relief valve is adjusted, you probably have a leak in the system somewhere. (Check all the hoses for deterioration and all the connections for tightness.) Low suction can also be accounted for by restrictions in the oil separator or pump discharge line. (The suction gauge itself could be bad, but that's rare.)

Over time, as the filters in your vacuum sytem become clogged with dust and debris, your suction-gauge readings will gradually increase: this is normal. (With some types of suction gauges, dirty filters will cause *less*-than-normal suction indications.) One thing you definitely want to watch out for, however, is *abnormally* high suction (5.5 inches or more, for most planes). Initially, high suction will cause your gyro instruments to react with unusual sensitivity—something you may enjoy. Ultimately, though, your gyros will react with total lunacy—something you won't enjoy at all (especially if you're in cloud).Higher-than-allowable suction gauge readings are usually the result of a clogged relief valve screen. The relief valve works this way:

In a wet-pump system, an air-oil separator must be used to return excess pump oil to the engine.

At low engine rpm, the vacuum pump is developing very little suction and the relief valve is closed.

As engine rpm picks up, suction increases dramatically, and the relief valve—which acts as a "controlled leak" in the system—opens. (If it *didn't* open, the vacuum pump would collapse the instrument lines at high engine power settings. Thus the term *relief* valve.)

The function of the relief valve, in other words, is to let extra air (unfiltered cabin air) into the system to keep the suction from becoming too great at normal engine operating speeds.

Obviously, then, if the relief valve becomes clogged at its screened opening, system suction will "mysteriously" increase—perhaps to the point of gyro malfunction. (Consult your aircraft manual for valve-screen cleaning instructions. The cleaning operation is simple and legal for pilots under FAR Part 43, but the procedures vary from installation to installation.)) If you understand the foregoing paragraphs, you know more about vacuum system maintenance than 99 percent of all pilots (and maybe 15 percent of all mechanics). Now go out and buy yourself a nice gift with the $100 or so you won't be spending on vacuum system (and gyro instrument) repairs over the next couple of years.

SERVICING THE AIR-OIL SEPARATOR

If they have wet-type vacuum pumps, most pilots don't give the air-oil separator much thought. For the most part, these innocuous little baffle-filled cannisters—which you'll find next to wet vacuum pumps and/or crankcase breather lines—go about their job quietly and reliably, year after year, their job being, of course, to *separate* air from oil, venting the former overboard and returning the latter to the crankcase. Occasionally, however, air-separators (or "filtrators," as they're sometimes dubbed) do go amuck. What happens is that the constant flow of air and oil causes the little cylinders to get gummy inside, so that eventually they clog to the point where the incoming air *and oil* would rather escape overboard, out the air-discharge line, than go their separate ways. The net result is that your engine suddenly becomes an oil exporter. Oil (from your vacuum pump or crankcase breather) goes out the vent line and onto the belly of your plane—and the next thing you know, you're scratching you head and asking yourself why the heck your engine has started to use so much oil.

If your plane has a wet-type vacuum pump and your oil consumption is up, or the underside of your plane is oily, this could be the reason. Your air-oil separator may well be clogged.

Cleaning the air-oil separator is *supposed* to be a once-a-year operation. Our experience has shown, however, that this little job very often doesn't get done at annual inspection time. Reason enough for you to go ahead and do it yourself *between* annuals (preferably once every 100 hours). The procedure is quite simple. And since FAR Part 43 allows you to replace "any hose connection except hydraulic connections," the whole thing qualifies under the FAA's preventive-maintenance rules. Here's all you do:

Separator Removal

First, locate your separator and note how it is installed. Look for a little black cannister; it will be somewhere near your vacuum pump at the rear of the engine. You'll see that there are three hoses leading to the unit: one to carry lubricating oil from the vacuum pump to the separator, one from the separator to the engine, and a discharge line leading to the bottom of the cowling. (If you've ever wondered what becomes of all the air that your vacuum pump sucks out of your cockpit, there's your answer. It goes out that long discharge line.

To free the separator, merely loosen the screw-clamps on the air/ oil-in hose, the oil-out hose, and the air-out hose, and unscrew or detach any mounting bracket that may be holding the separator in place. Be sure to identify those three hoses in some positive way so you'll be able to hook them up correctly on reassembly.

Next, carry your separator over to a work bench or solvent sink, drop it in a can of Varsol or Stoddard solvent or shop naphtha—and go have lunch.

Reinstallation

After lunch, pull your filtrator out of the solvent bath, shake it vigorously, pour the contents out, and resubmerge the cannister once more. Repeat this cycle four or five times, or until the solvent rinse comes clear. Blow out the cleaned separator with compressed air, or shake well and air dry.

Now you can reinstall the separator on the aircraft. You may, at this point, notice a small restrictor in the oil return line to the engine; whatever you do, *don't* use a pointed object of any sort to clean deposits out of this orifice. You mustn't enlarge this hole.

While reinstalling the separator in its previous position, check the condition of all hoses and clamps, replacing any questionable components with new parts. When you're done, run the engine up and reinspect the area for oil leaks. If no leaks are found, make your log entry (so you'll know when your next filtrator cleaning is due).

And don't be surprised if your engine suddenly starts "exporting" less oil.

DRY VACUUM PUMPS: FAILURES AND REPLACEMENT

The modern dry vacuum pump—when it works—is an impressive technical accomplishment. Economical ($200 to $400), low-weight (under three pounds), and capable of high-rpm, high-output operation, the dry pump has totally displaced its traditional competition (venturis and oil-lubricated "wet" pumps) in a matter of only a few years, making possible IFR panels for essentially all light aircraft. If the dry pump has a hitch (and it does), it is that—as the FAA said in a recent letter to the National Transportation Safety Board "pumps fail catastrophically, without warning, and there is no degradation of performance obvious to the pilot to warn him of imminent failure.

On the Inside

To understand why pumps fail, it is helpful to know something about pump anatomy. We autopsied a couple of failed pumps (obtained from an FBO's trash barrel) to see how the pumps are constructed. Both Airborne and Edo (now Sigma-Tec) pumps utilize carbon-graphite rotor construction, with carbon vanes riding loose in the rotor slots. In normal operation, the vanes are thrown against the pump housing by centrifugal force, rising and falling on the elliptical walls and thus compressing the air trapped in the vaned compartments. The Edo rotor has eight slots and eight vanes; it can be turned in either direction. The Airborne design, by contrast, uses six slots and vanes, each at a slight angle, giving the pump a preferred direction of rotation. Airborne units thus come in "CW" (clockwise) and "CC" (counterclockwise) models, and for long life, the proper polarity must be observed on installation.

In either case—Edo or Airborne—the vanes run dry on the aluminum housing walls; the constant, gradual wearing away of the graphite is the only lubrication the pump gets. Hence the term "dry pump."

Note also, incidentally, that dry pumps can be used to suck air (provide vacuum) or blow air (provide positive pressure), depending on which side you hook the plumbing to. When dry pumps are used to provide pressure (as in deice boot systems), inline filters must be employed to remove carbon dust from the system.

Both Edo and Airborne pumps have a standard AND20000 spline-drive mounting for use on Lycoming or Continental accessory cases. Also both Edo and Airborne incorporate frangible drive couplings, which are designed to shear in the event of rotor lockup, thus sparing the engine accessory gears of possible damage. It's apparent, however, that the pump makers differ in their approach to drive coupling design: Edo's coupling transmits torque straight to the rotor along a thin quill-shaft (which has since been changed to a speedometer-type cable in the so-called "dash three" pump models). Airborne, on the other hand, transmits drive torque to the rotor via a somewhat complicated coupling sandwiching eight shear pins between a nylon torque plate and an upper torque plate, with the rotor spinning on three finger spools which "grab into" the rotor at about the half-radius point.

If it sounds like the Edo (or Sigma-Tec) pump drive is "more frangible" than the stouter (if more complex) Airborne nylon-torque-plate drive, you're right. The Edo quill-shaft is designed to fail at 100 inch-pounds of torque, whereas it takes more than twice as much torque (250 inch-pounds) to snap an Airborne drive. Accordingly, one often finds Edo pumps failing due to drive-coupling breakage not associated with rotor lockup or vane distress.

One Airborne pump we know of suffered real internal damage before its nylon drive sheared. At least one of the vanes apparently broke in service. When that happens, odd-shaped bits of carbon can wedge between the rotor and housing wall, jamming the rotor. The pump we autopsied showed several broken vanes and deep rotor cracks as well, probably induced by the sudden shock of stoppage. As you can imagine, even experts can have a tough time pinpointing the primary cause of a given pump failure.

A Complex of Causes

What causes pumps to fail? Suffice it to say, *no one thing*. The use of carbon graphite as a structural—as well as a lubricating—material in these pumps certainly seems intrinsic to the problem. And yet, ironically, it's carbon graphite's unique qualities that make current "self-lubed" pump designs possible in the first place.

In our research (which included talking to the two major pump manufacturers as well as mechanics, owners, and overhaulers), we have identified no fewer than ten things that could cause a dry pump to self-destruct:

1. Solvent Contamination

Oil or oil vapor rapidly contaminates carbon graphite, turning the lubricating powder at the rubbing surface into a hostile sludge. Oil from the aircraft engine can enter the pump via several routes: a bad pump mounting gasket, oil blown rearward from the crankcase breather drawn into the pump by its own suction. Another cause of contamination-failure is entry into the pump of degreasing solvent (the type sprayed on the engine for routine inspections). Unless exceptional care is taken, Varsol can enter a pump through its exhaust tube or drive seals. Obviously, this is something to watch for during any engine spray-down.

2. Foreign Object Ingestion

Carbon graphite is brittle and quite fragile. A small sliver of rubber hose (liberated by wiggling the plumbing during pump installation), or even the carbon bits left in the lines by a previous pump, can cause immediate failure. Generally this type of failure occurs shortly after installation of a new pump. Pump manufacturers lay the blame for a large percentage of warranty claims to this cause.

It should be noted that even airborne dust is sufficient to give most dry pumps fits. (A filter change is usually required for warranty coverage to be in effect after installing a new pump.) There is also some concern that particles small enough to *pass through* filters can mix with the lubricating powder at the rubbing sufaces of the vane and rotor, increasing the wear rate and leading to early pump failure. Cigarette smoke contains particles small enough to pass through filters, and, of course, in planes with suction-operated gyros, cabin air is the starting point for pump-pickup airflow.

3. Drive Misalignment

One of the more controversial (with manufacturers) aspects of the pump-life problem is a parallel misalignment of spline-drive gears caused by "engine drive gears not being where Continental says they are" (in the words of one pump engineer). Poor pump lineup was reportedly one of the reasons EDO/Sigma-Tec went to a speedo-cable-type drive "shaft" on its 1U128A-03 pump. Substantial efforts are continuing at the manufacturer level in designing more compliant drive mechanisms which (manufacturers say privately) should help pumps cope better with misalignments that can be as much as ten times worse than expected from published engine specifications.

4. Heat and Altitude Stress

The heat of compression developed in a dry pump operating at or near full output is of the same order of magnitude as that produced by a turbocharger. And the higher you fly, the harder the pump works. At 22,000 feet, a 2111/212 Airborne pump develops a "delta-P" of 11 inches of mercury, maximum (up to 22 inches for a 441-series pump), which means internal temperatures can easily exceed 200°F. Cooling is usually very poor—in part because of low humidity at high altitudes and in part because aircraft designers often neglect to expose the vacuum pump to ram air, instead sequestering it in a "dead spot" behind the engine baffling (where temperatures are already high.)

Concerned about the increase in turbo traffic at the middle flight levels, the National Transportation Safety Board in 1982 specifically asked the FAA to evaluate the reliability of small dry pumps at high cruise altitudes, but the FAA's efforts since then have been limited to "monitoring manufacturer testing, (which has so far) proved inconclusive." Pamco Industries, the Milwaukee-based pump overhauler, has tested the 211CC Airborne pump in the up mode (i.e., powering gyros only) at altitudes to 30,000 feet, where it performed satisfactorily. But nobody really knows what the reliability of dry pumps is at high altitudes. For most installations, testing simply hasn't been done.

5. Overspeed

Exceeding engine redline is another proven method for trashing your vacuum pump. Most pumps begin to provide usable suction (or pressure) around 1,500 rpm and provide optimal life at engine rpms below 2,000. (Not surprisingly, this is the speed chosen by designers of electrically powered backup pump systems.) The maximum continuous operating speed of Airborne pumps is 4,000 rpm (rotor shaft); for Edo pump, 4,200 rpm. Lycoming pump pads generally turn 1.3 times crankshaft speed. Continental pump pads, however, turn 1.5 to 1.545 times crank speed, which means that any time a Continental operator's engine rpm exceeds 2,588, the Airborne pump limits are being busted; and any time a Continental owner turns up more than 2,700 rpm, Edo's rpm limits are violated. Combine high rpm with high demand (as in a Continental-powered Cessna P210 with deice boots flying at 20,000 feet), and you can begin to see why some operators experience so many problems with pumps. Add a bonafide prop overspeed incident to the scenario (whether intentional or unintentional), and you've got real trouble.

6. Rapid Acceleration

Rapid engine acceleration (on a go-around, for example) can apparently put unusual loads on the rotor and vanes, which may be why test-stand pumps often run trouble-free for many hundreds of hours, while operators in the field continue to rack up unexplainable premature failures. Whether the acceleration problem is strictly one of mechanical stress, or also involves thermal shock, is anyone's guess at the moment.

7. Reverse Rotation

As mentioned earlier, Airborne pumps come in clockwise (CW) and counterclockwise (CC) flavors, designed to rotate in one and only one direction. The profile of the elliptical rotor bore is not symmetrical in an Airborne pump; also, the rotor slots are cut at an angle. (These design features may improve performance, but some experts feel they make the carbon rotor more susceptible to damage.) Attention to label instructions can eliminate incorrect rotation of pumps in normal use, but avoiding occasional engine "kickback" on startup (or shutdown) is not such an easy matter yet if vane/slot clearances have opened up, one kickback may be all that's needed to jam a rotor and trash a pump. Pamco Industries' Thomas Zompolas (designer of a new standby vacuum system for Mooneys) says pumps used as standbys tend to last longer than the same pumps installed on engines. "That's why you often hear guys say, 'But it was working fine when I shut down' " Zompolas maintains.

8. Rough Handling

The FAA's Service Difficulty Report file abounds with examples of "fresh out of the box" pump failures, where just spinning the drive shaft by hand is found to be enough to lock up the rotor. Assuming (and we do) that the manufacturers exercise a modicum of quality control, what could be the explanation? One likely cause is transit "ship-shock," which can jar vanes enough to chip a corner (or cause other mischief). Of course, pumps also respond poorly to having their housings squeezed in a vise (which is something many A&Ps do while installing fittings in the inlet/outlet holes of a new pump, against the express warnings of the manufacturers), being dropped on the floor, etc.—but your mechanic never does such things ... right?

It's interesting to note that floatplane operators (who suffer a relatively high incidence of shock-related avionics and panel problems) have reported replacing vacuum pumps every 50 to 200 hours, on average—further evidence that mere shock and vibration can have a profoundly destructive effect on pumps.

9. Pump Lugging

A recent focus on pump failures in Cessna 210 wing boots has tended to underscore the fact that deice boots place a heavy burden on vacuum boots—ultimately detracting from reliability. Whether the erosion of reliability is simply due to the higher average pump loads or to other factors, is not clear. The FAA has received Service Difficulty Reports describing sticking deice boot valves in some aircraft. Ordinarily, pneumatic deice boots cycle on and off, alternately inflating and deflating, at the behest of a small timer and solenoid-actuated deice boot flow valve. If either the timer or the valve hangs up in the "inflate" position, however, the vacuum pump can quickly lug and overheat. Until recently, the loss of a vacuum pump in this manner meant not only the loss of boot action, but gyro instruments as well. But the NTSB has explicitly called for independent instrument power sources as a requirement for deicing certification. Meanwhile, owners of boot-equipped aircraft should be aware of the role of timers and flow valves in possible vacuum pump problems.

10. Normal Wear

Dry pumps inevitably wear out (nothing made of graphite lasts forever), and—quite naturally—if it is left in service long enough, any dry pump is eventually going to stop working just from its vanes rubbing down to nothingness. The question is, how long should a pump last? According to overhaulers' figures, under the best of circumstances, smaller (211-type) dry pumps are unlikely to operate reliably over 600 hours, as the vanes will have worn to the point where they are likely to cock and jam. (By contrast, makers of electrically driven standby pumps systems are confident that the same pumps—if they are protected from heat, vibrations, overspeed, contamination, etc.—can be counted on to run 1,000 hours or more.) By all accounts,

Pressure regulator valve (note safety-wired head) is easily visible in late-model Bonanzas. The area at the base of the valve should be checked visually for excess carbon at each preflight. Rapid carbon buildup is indicative of pump distress.

the so-called "boot pumps"(high capacity Airbornes) are unlikely, in most applications, to last more than 300 to 400 hours. Of course, there are always exceptions.

In short, then, the modern dry pump, by virtue of its design and construction, is acutely sensitive to almost everything in its normal environment: heat, oil, solvents, dirt, water, vibration, mechanical stress, and (some would say) the moon and tides. Even under the best of circumstances—with a new pump installed by experts, with cleaned lines and filters, with adequate protection from solvents and oil, and with your striving to keep your throttle applications smooth and your landings soft—you still cannot expect much more than three years of normal flying before your pump (whether Brand A or Brand E) fails.

The only thing certain is that it *will* fail. You just can't say when.

Detecting Imminent failure

What if your pump is on the verge of giving out? Is there a way to tell? Do you have to wait until the artifical horizon rolls over dead to learn that your vacuum pump has pumped its last breath? There are ways to detect and guard against the onset of failure.

First, on every preflight (if your cowl is openable), you should get into the habit of visually inspecting not only your vacuum pump, but the pressure relief valve or exhaust tube. Look for two things at the pump: the presence of oil at the base of the flange (indicating a bad gasket) and the accumulation of tiny bits of stripped nylon in the coupling area (which is open for view—although you must look closely). Bits of nylon are a sure indication that the coupling is fretting in preparation for outright failure. Be forewarned.

In a pressure-type system, give the relief valve (in the firewall area) a visual once-over periodically. Look for carbon buildup (i.e., black soot) indicating possible rotor/vane distress. By checking the regulator filter—or the downstream inline filter—at set intervals, you can get an idea of the normal soot buildup produced by your pump due to normal wear. Abnormal buildups will then be easy to detect.

In the cockpit, learn to include the pressure of suction gauge in your normal visual scan. And take the gauge seriously. In a dry-pump system, any rapid fluctation of the gauge (no matter how intermittent) is a definite warning signal that something is amiss. See that your system is properly adjusted to give the correct handbook readings at 1,500 rpm or above. (Most regulators don't begin to regulate until 1,500.)

Airborne has for years offered a Pneumatic Source Indicator (Model 344) that shows the pilot, by means of a fluorescent red ball in a tiny indicator, whether the vacuum pump has failed—in effect, a vacuum-source "idiot light" (although the annunciator is not electric). But if your plane already has a suction gauge, there really is no reason to install the Airborne PSI. Again: Start to include the suction gauge in your scan.

Dual vacuum pump installations have received a lot of attention, what with Cessna's experiences with the 210 series. Unfortunately, not every small-plane engine has an extra AND20000 pad available for a standby pump, and while the engine manufacturers have developed T-drive adaptors for some applications, the drives are not widely retrofittable.

Still, if you want a standby vacuum pump in your system (and you don't want to trade up to a twin), there are ways to do it. Two companies now offer remoted, electrically-driven (with a small DC motor) standby vacuum pumps for retrofit to single-engine aircraft. Electro-Mech, of Wichita, KS, and Aerosafe Inc., of Dallas,TX, both market systems using an electrically driven Airborne pump (switchable by the pilot) to provide backup vacuum or pressure in the event of primary pump failure.

Vacuum Pump Replacement Checklist

Replacing a vacuum pump need not be a major hassle, if you follow a rational sequence of procedures. Here is a checklist for guidance:

1. Troubleshoot Cause(s) of Last Pump Failure

Booted aircraft: Check for normal deice timer operation. Timer should inflate boots for approximately six seconds (somewhat variable in pressure-dependent deice systems, but should not exceed 15 seconds for any one cycle). Boots should be pressure bleed-down checked for leaks using Airborne 343 Test Kit. Inflatable door seals: Check that the system inflates and holds pressure without recycling (no leaks). Pneumatic autopilots: Check autopilot regulators, servos, and filters per manufacturer's specifications. Other systems: Check pneumatic camera doors, avionics cooling, etc., per aircraft service manual.

2. Replace all system filters

Failure to change filters may void new pump warranties. Pump inlet filters (pressure systems) and garters (suction) should be replaced once a year or every 100 hours. Central gyro filters should be replaced once a year or every 500 hours (ditto for auxiliary inline filters).

3. Verify correct replacement pump P/N

Do not merely replace existing pump with identical-part-number item. Consult aircraft Parts Catalog or pump maker's Application List. Also (if using an Airborne pump) conduct a rotation check: Remove old pump, then manually rotate propeller in normal direction while drive pad gear is observed. (Observe proper safety precautions when turning propeller.) If drive gear rotates clockwise, a "CW" pump should be specified. If counterclockwise, order a "CC" pump.

4. Remove old pump and gasket

Your old pump (even if damaged) has salvage value; many pump overhaulers will pay $20 or more to have it. Do not reuse old gaskets. New pumps should be mounted on the new gaskets that accompany them.

5. Remove fittings from old pump

Discard stripped or damaged fittings, fittings with rounded wrench flats, etc. Thoroughly clean and dry serviceable new fittings before using them.

6. Install fittings in new pump

Here, it is permissible to clamp the new pump in a vise *at the base flange only* (never at the center housing). Spray clean fittings with *silicone lube* and *allow to dry* before screwing them in by hand. *Do not use Teflon tape, pipe dope, or unapproved thread lubes.* Tighten fittings down one and a half turns maximum, using a *box wrench.* Align fittings as appropriate for plumbing connections in aircraft.

7. Check the AND20000 drive pad for oil

The pad should be dry, with no oil leaking out. Replace pad seal if necessary.

8. Install new pump

Be sure to lay the gasket in place first, then install the pump. *If you drop the pump, discard it.* (Likewise, if the pump shows obvious signs of damage, exchange it for another one.) Replace all locking devices. Cinch all four mounting nuts alternately to 50 inch-pounds minimum, 70 inch-pounds maximum.

9. Install hoses

Inspect hoses inside and out for contamination, condition, etc., and

Typical air filter in an AN-style gyro is held in by a snap ring. The filter element is merely a sandwich of wire screen-paper-wire screen, stapled together at the center. It's a snap to replace the paper element.

replace questionable hoses. (Replace brittle or aged hoses to avoid separation of inner layers of hose, which can break loose during handling and be ingested by the pump, leading to premature failure.) In a pressure system that has experienced pump failure, be sure to *blow out all lines* with compressed air *from the panel side*, to remaining bits of carbon. Make sure hoses are connected to the *proper fittings* (do not swap inlet/outlet hoses by mistake).

10. Check pressure/suction regulation
Run engine to 1,500 rpm and check that suction gauge is reading in the green (or per manual specs).

[Note to Airborne customers: Airborne specifies a life limit of six years for nylon drive couplings. Factory kits are available for replacing couplings: Kit No. 350 for 211/212 series pumps, No. 352 for 440-series pumps. See your dealer for details or write Airborne Division, Parker Hannifin, 711 Taylor St., Elyria, OH 44035.]

HANDLING FILTERS
AND GYRO INSTRUMENTS
Inspecting and Replacing Filters

If your gyro instruments are on a common manifold with a common filter, a low-vacuum indication is normally due to a dirty filter. Don't adjust the vacuum relief valve until you have eliminated all the other possibilities.

Changing the filter is best begun by studying the instructions that come with the new elements.

There are two types of filtration. Older airplanes have built-in filters on their old AN gyros. To get at them usually requires that the instruments be removed, unless you have long arms and are into masochism. Filters are simple affairs: a sandwich of filter paper stapled between two pieces of window screen.

Should you be unable to find standard replacements (they are becoming a bit of a rarity), the staples can be removed and fresh filter paper (see your local druggist) can be inserted and trimmed, and the sandwich restapled. FAR Part 21 allows you to do this.

The other prevailing filter system is the central cannister type filter, with a manifold to the vacuum instruments. These are easily replaced. Trace out the lines from the backs of the gauges until you find the filter (it may be an unusual location; on the P210, for instance, it's outside the fuselage, in the left wing root); then remove the snap ring or worm clamp and replace the element. (Most FBOs stock these elements.)

In both cases, the more difficult the access, the more likely the filters will have been missed by maintenance personnel during inspections (although filter replacement is often *required* for warranties to be effective after gyro or dry-pump replacement).

Removing and Reinstalling Gyro Instruments

If an instrument overhaul is called for, remove the instruments' fittings and store them in a safe place, as they are often lost during overhaul or exchange.

If the gauges can be caged before shipping, do so—and pack everything as carefully as you can (label the container "Fragile as Eggs"). Any sharp rap of a gyroscopic instrument is enough to damage the bearing races, a catastrophy to longevity.

After overhaul and reinstallation, note that in most cases there are slotted screw holes for both the turn coordinator and artifical horizon. The best way to proceed is to look in the aircraft service manual (or ask your avionics or instrument technician) and find out how to level the aircraft about its roll axis. In many cases, technicians simply lay a bubble level across the seat rails laterally, then let air out of one of the other main tire until the plane is level.

After levelling the plane on the ramp, start the engine and get the vacuum up to its normal operating range; then level the artificial horizon and center the turn coordinator's ball between the lines. Then, finally, cinch everything in place. (Do this in conjunction with rigging the controls, and you'll no longer be among the appalling majority of pilots who fly one wing low. Instrument flying will now be a comparative breeze, and your plane may actually pick up a knot or two in cruise.)

Keep in mind that many autopilots' computers are hooked to the gyroscopic instruments; from them, you will have a collection of cannon plugs and wires. Don't forget to reconnect them after an instrument overhaul.

PITOT-STATIC PROTECTION

From the beginning of flight training, pilots are sternly warned: Let nothing block the pitot tube or static ports of your airplane, lest terrible things occur. Yet such disasters do occur to airplanes ranging from J-

Caging adjustment, with special tool, is found underneath AN-style gyro.

3s to jetliners. Blocked pitot-static systems can so distort airspeed and altitude readings that unthinking pilots allow themselves to be deceived into terminally stalling out or diving into the ground.

Ground and Air Defenses

Blockage occurs through many agents: foreign solid objects such as insects, dirt, and other things, as well as water, including that major culprit, ice. Static ports can also be blocked by foreign matter—or even mistakenly be waxed or painted over.

In the air, the pilot should know how to interpret incongruous instrument readings and what safe control responses to make, as we shall see. Often, he or she need only activate the pitot heat (when in— better still, when approaching—cloud or precipitation in near- or below-freezing OAT) or the alternate static air source. However, the first safety measures should be taken on the ground through careful preflighting and protecting the pitot tube and static ports from contamination between flights.

Pitot tubes are particularly vulnerable to the mischief of those who know not or care not what they do to the system—bugs, and even people, who have been known to use the pitot tube to dispose of gum or gum wrapper. To thwart such sabotage, buy or make pitot tube covers to keep mud daubers, leaf-cutter bees, and other hot-weather insects from nesting in the pitot tube orifice. (The first heat wave of the season triggers most such critters to mate—and nest.) Pitot covers come in various types. You want to avoid the slip-on types that fit snugly, as these can cause pressure spikes in the pitot system on installation and removal. (If you doubt this, watch your airspeed indicator as someone jams on and pulls off the cover.) Old spark-plug ship tubes—with red streamers attached—make good pitot covers (the price is certainly right), as do bright-red baby booties Or you can be bourgeois and order one of the many readymade pitot covers offered by the mail-order outlets.

Protect the pitot-static system from water. (Also, drain and/or blow out the system periodically.)

A plugged pitot is a fairly obvious source of mayhem; if you don't catch it on preflight, you'll notice it about halfway into your takeoff roll, as the ASI fails to spool up. A blocked static system, however, is far more insidious. On takeoff, the ASI will read normally until well after liftoff, but as the climb begins, the airspeed indication will start to decay (even with normal deck angles and climb power settings). The altimeter remains at field elevation, and the ROC stays at zero. Visualize, if you will, taking off into a low overcast, then glancing down at these readings; the typical reaction is to dive to attempt to regain "flying speed." The proper reaction is to hold deck angle, then turn on the alternate static system (which commonly vents to the cabin, on unpressurized aircraft).

One such incident occured to the pilot of a late-model Cessna 310. After takeoff, he noticed that the climb rate and airspeed were not anywhere near normal for the prevailing temperature and gross weight. When he levelled off, the airspeed crawled up to normal, and the altimeter continued to seem sluggish. He turned on the autopilot and was greeted with odd pitch excursions. Figuring out the problem—the static system was partially blocked—he turned on the alternate static source and flew home, to learn from the owner that someone had waxed the airplane over the weekend. The static ports had been partially blocked with the stuff.

Another case of pilot uncertainty was potentially more lethal. This took place during a checkout of a new captain. The check pilot relates, "The weather was down to landing minimums (1,800 RVR) and the runway was slick, the airport having undergone a seige of blowing, freezing rain. The new captain was riding shotgun in the co-pilot's seat. He took off normally, transitioning almost instantly to instruments. Then, as his airspeed indication eroded and the airplane refused to climb, he began screaming for more power. In turn, I guarded the yoke so he didn't start to dive, and told him—in an equally vocal command—to turn on his alternate static system. Any pilot who flies IFR should be able to find any switch in the cockpit, blindfolded, on the darkest night. He reached out and actutated the alternate static without hesitation. That's my kind of guy."

Pitot heat is often neglected in such emergencies, the alternate static system even more so. When ice strikes and the gauges start to go even mildly berserk, keep both devices very much in mind and use.

Checking the Static System

Under FAR 91. 171, for instrument flight, the static system must be checked every 24 months. The procedure and required equipment are uncomplicated enough that any fairly adept owner can do the job in about ten minutes. With an A&P's signoff, such maintenance is legal.

The first thing you do is zip on down to the pharmacy or medical supply house, and buy one of those rubber air bulbs—called Baumanometer bulbs—you commonly see used with blood-pressure cuffs. (There are other types as well.)

You'll also need a short length of thick-walled tubing (such as Tygon-type or surgical tubing) and a hose clamp, which are obtainable at any auto or motorcycle parts store. A jar of petroleum jelly wouldn't be a bad idea, either. Also, depending on where your plane's static port is, you may need an assistant to help out in the cockpit.

Before beginning the static test, go inside the cockpit and make sure that the "alternate static source" valve is *off*; if your plane has a static-system drain, drain the system.

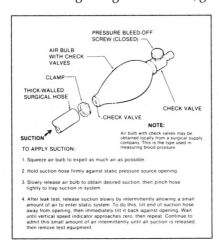

If your plane has two interconnected static ports (one on each side of the fuselage—a common arrangement for counteracting the effects of sideslipping), carefully seal off one port with tape. This seal must be air-tight, but use care not to foul the port with dirt or gum.

Couple the short piece of

surgical tubing to the Baumanometer bulb securely, using a hose clamp, and apply a small amount of petroleum jelly to the open end of the hose (which should be cut off very squarely so that it will mate flatly to the side of the airplane). The idea is to stick the hose over the static port (holding it there with firm hand pressure) to make a temporary air-tight seal, and then to pump the suction bulb to create a partial vacuum in the airplane static system. While you're doing this, somebody—preferably you—must watch the airplane's *airspeed indicator, altimeter*, and *VSI/rate-of-climb indicator*. Continue squeezing the Baumanometer bulb until an indicated altitude of 1,000 to 2,000 feet (AGL) is shown, but *monitor the ASI and VSI to prevent suction "spikes" that could damage those instruments*. (In no case do you want to exceed the travel limits of the airspeed or ROC indicators.)

Once the altimeter is showing a couple grand, stop pumping and hold fast on the suction. There should be no leaks, and the VSI should hold steady at or close to zero. Cessna's shop manuals allow a rate of leakage of 100 fpm (measured by the altimeter and a stopwatch). Anything more than that suggests a bad hose clamp or leaky instrument somewhere in the system. (Troubleshooting this situation is fairly easy—all you do is disconnect the common static lines from the VSI, altimeter, and ASI, and reconnect the altimeter into the static system, then repeat the leakdown test as necessary to identify the faulty gauge. Alternatively, with the VSI, ASI, and autopilot plumbing capped off and isolated from the static system, apply *pressure* to the static system until the altimeter "descends" 500 feet or more, then paint suspect hose connections with soap fluid to find the leaker.) At the end of the test, admit air back into the system *slowly* so as not to damage delicate instrument mechanisms.

Sounds pretty easy, and it is. Just remember that any time *any* static-system connection is broken—for any reason—the basic static check *must* be repeated and entered into the plane's logs (read FAR 91.171). Also remember that for IFR flight, a separate *altimeter* check must be done—by an approved instrument shop, not an A&P. The static check, however, is one check any A&P can do legally—which also means you can do it legally, with a signoff.

Chapter 3

ENGINE INSTRUMENTS

The kind of flying that our equipment allows us to do today means greater operational freedom, but it also calls for more knowledge of our powerplants and their instrumentation. Knowing what the instruments say can be crucial to safety, for an ailing engine most often begins to warn of problems during flight. Engine warning signs are discussed at length in our Light Plane Maintenance Library volumes on powerplants. Our emphasis here is on familiarity with the instruments themselves and ways of keeping them well maintained.

AN INSTRUMENT LITERACY CHALLENGE

As a service to help you to determine how well you understand the instruments in your panel, we will make a slight deviation by offering a quick test to provide you with an indication of weak areas in your instrument "literacy." As you ponder the questions and the answers that immediately follow them, consider: How well do you know your power system? How well do you understand the messages of your

plane's instruments? What idiosyncratic indication should you account for as you fly?

These questions are certainly not exhaustive, but, if you are honest with yourself in trying to answer them, they may reveal significant things about the state of your knowledge. The answers should also provide useful operational information.

It pays to study your power instruments (CHT, EGT,MP, oil temp, etc.)—not only in the air, but on the ground. A check of your own plane's engine-gauge installation may reveal some interesting idiosyncracies, perhaps not readily apparent even from a reading of the service manual.

For example: Do you know where the oil-pressure pickoff point is on your engine? The CHT pickoff? Oil temp?

Is your CHT probe a thermocouple or a thermistor?

Perhaps you already feel pretty knowledgeable concerning the engine instruments. In that case, you should have no trouble with the following quiz:

1. (True or False) If you turn your master switch off, your EGT will go dead.

2. Of the oil-temperature indicator, cylinder head temp (CHT) gauge, and oil pressure gauge, which one is not "required equipment" for VFR flight?

3. (True or False) On airplanes that use a Bourdon-tube movement in the oil-temp indicator, a break in the Bourdon tube would allow crankcase oil to squirt into the cockpit.

4. If a short circuit in your fuel-quantity indication system blows that circuit breaker, you will lose—in addition to fuel quantity indications— which of the following?

(a.) The CHT, oil temp, and oil pressure.

(b.) The CHT only.

(c.) The fuel pressure indicator.

(d.) None of the above.

5. Under normal cruise conditions, in a carbureted airplane, application of carburetor heat will cause the EGT to (choose one) go up, go down, not change.

6. (True or False) After a battery-draining hard start attempt, CHT indications—once airborne—are likely to be 25 to 50 degrees high for the first part of the flight.

7. Although the compression is good, the intercylinder EGT spread on your fuel injected engine has widened noticeably, the spark plugs

are oily, power is down slightly, and fuel flow is up. These are classical indications of:
    (a.) Advanced ring blowby.
    (b.) Malfunctioning fuel pump.
    (c.) Dirty injector nozzles.
    (d.) Detonation.
    8. On a standard day (50°F , 29.92 inches Hg) at sea level, with the engine stopped, your manifold pressure gauge reads 28.00 inches. In flight, your MP gauge will read
    (a.) About two inches too low.
    (b.) About two inches too high.
    (c.) Fairly accurately.
    (d.) Impossible to say without more information.
    9. (True or False) In a turbocharged airplane, manifold pressure and deck pressure are essentially the same.
    10. (True or False) If an analog-type fuel-flow gauge breaks, fuel can enter the cockpit.
    Now for the answers:
    Number One is a trick question. Digital EGTs will of course go dead the instant the master switch is flicked off. But *so will majority of top-line EGTs,* which utilize power amplification of the signal from their thermocouple probes. Many older EGTs are non-amplified and will continue to display information after an electrical disablement. Do you know which type of instrument your plane has?
    Two: FAR 91.33 requires all but the cylinder head temperature gauge for VFR flight.
    Three: Although newer aircraft use a thermistor probe to measure oil temperature, most pre-1980 single-engine planes employ a closed-capillary oil-temp sensing mechanism, with a curled tube (a *Bourdon tube*) at the needle movement. If the tube breaks, the capillary will vent ammonia (or whatever capillary fluid happens to be used) to the cockpit; but since the capillary forms a closed bulb at the engine end, no oil can enter it. (Your *oil pressure* line, on the other hand, *is* connected to the engine's oil system and will fill with oil in the event of a sender-tube break.)
    Four: "b" is correct for most aircraft, although it varies. The engine instrument cluster, which contains the fuel gauges in many aircraft, is commonly wired to a single circuit breaker. Unless your CHT is of the spark plug thermocouple type (very rare nowadays), chances are good you'll lose CHT when your fuel-gauge CB pops. Check your

plane"s wiring diagrams closely. In some aircraft, the CHT and fuel gauges are gang-wired through the landing gear light circuit breaker (Cessna 210G) or through an accessory CB. In others, the fuel gauges and CHT each have their own separate CBs (P210).

Five: Application of carb heat causes the mixture to enrichen and EGT to go down, under most conditions. (Try it and you'll see.)

Six: True. In a thermistor-type CHT system (as is used virtually all post-Eisenhower aircraft), the instrument movement actually consists of a voltmeter or ohmmeter, calibrated in degrees Fahrenheit instead of volts or ohms. The readout will vary with line voltage (and hence charge rate). When the charge rate is high—as following a hard start—system voltage may be as much as 10 percent higher than normal, until the battery has come back up. Ten percent of the CHT scale is about 30°. Under high-charge-rate conditions, CHT may thus read 30° high. (Conversely, under low-system-voltage conditions, CHT will read falsely low.)

Seven: "c" (dirty injector nozzles). The fact that compression is good rules out ring blowby as the culprit, and there is no way a defective fuel pump can effect a change in EGT *spread*. (Detonation, in and of itself, causes no change in fuel flow, nor does it leave oil on spark plugs.) That leaves *dirty injector nozzles* as the true culprit—the dead giveaway here being the high-fuel indication. (A careful check of *actual* fuel consumption will show a net decrease or no change at all.) Standard-equipment fuel-flow gauges are nothing but *pressure* indicators plumbed to the injector spider hub (or flow divider). When one or more nozzles plug up, back-pressure in the hub causes fuel-flow indications in the cockpit to *rise*. Power will lessen, and the engine may or may not run rough. The lessened combustion pressure typically allows oil to creep past rings, wetting the spark plugs. A well-intentioned A&P seeing these symptoms might rather hastily suggest a top overhaul. (Lycoming reports that engines have been returned to the factory with nothing wrong except plugged injector nozzles.) The canny aircraft owner, however, checks simple things first, before investing in major repairs. A nozzle wash job, in this case, is all that's indicated.

Eight: "a" is most correct. Granted, the gauge linearity is not perfect, and the exact amount of error will vary at different points on the scale, but it's nonetheless a fact that the gauge is indicating too low—it should read 29.92 inches with the engine stopped. On a turbocharged aircraft, it's likely you would be overboosting on takeoff.

Nine: False. Deck pressure refers to pressure ahead of the throttle plate (which, depending on the exact turbo installation, may be anywhere from two to 10 inches more than MP). Manifold pressure is always taken downstream of the throttle butterfly.

Ten: True. Indeed, every year the FAA receives several reports of raw fuel in the cockpit due to breakage of the fuel flow sense line. The line is usually actually void of fuel in normal operation, but when a break occurs, it fills rapidly.

Did you score all right answers? (If the FAA had included these questions in your last written test, would you have gotten at least seven of them right?) Consider your score an indication of how well you know the plane(s) you fly—and, perhaps, how much more you *could* know.

OIL PRESSURE GAUGES

Oil pressure and temperature indicators only frequently cause headaches by themselves, but oil systems have added pain to many an aircraft owner and pilot's existence. The instruments do sometimes fail, of course, and they need attention—particularly oil pressure gauges—if only because they do much to warn us if oil problems have developed.

Because the gauges and the overall system are so closely inter-related, it is important to be familiar with both. Oil pressure is something most low-time pilots give little thought to (you either have it or

Pro pilots know the oil gauges tell a continuing tale.

you don't, seems to be their attitude), but old-timers know that the oil-pressure gauge tells a story. Pro pilots include the gauge in their VFR scan (IFR,too), and monitor it on takeoff roll as well. It's an important instrument—and not in the idiot-light, all-or-nothing sense.

You may think you know your engine pretty well, but can you recall the exact location of the oil-pressure pickoff? (Can you name the major bearings and/or accessories located down-stream of the pickoff point?) Engine-makers try to locate the pressure pickoff as far down-stream of the oil pump in the lubrication loop as possible, but the exact location varies. For example, on the Continental O-300 series engines, the gauge pressure line is aft of cylinder number one. The O-470 has two possible pickoffs—one between cylinders two and four (the preferred spot) and another between jugs one and three (less used).

Oil Circulation

Do you know how the oil circulates in your particular engine? This is important information, too, and it varies from model to model.

In the sandcast-case Continental 520s, oil circulates through the engine in a counter clockwise fashion (looking down). Pressure oil from the oil pump proceeds from the filter (or pressure screen) up the right-side galleries to the front-mounted oil cooler, across the front of the engine to the prop governor, back down the left (port) side galleries (which feed the main bearings), and from the rear main bearings to the accessory drives. (This scheme holds also for the 470 series engine.)

In the Permold-case Continentals, oil proceeds from the oil pumps (and filter) to the rear-mounted oil cooler, from there branching off in several directions at once: to the crankshaft, left gallery (supplying the main bearings) and governor, and to the right gallery. (Left and right galleries normally supply the port and starboard lifters and rockers, with oil under tappet pressure flowing up the hollow pushrods, to the rockers, to valve stems via rocker squirt holes, and back to the sump through the pushrod shroud tubes—or through the rocker box drain tubes, in a Lycoming engine.)

Lycoming does things a little differently. On most models, the oil pressure pickoff is located on the accessory case just above the right magneto (about four o'clock to the vacuum pump drive pad, looking from the cockpit). On some, it's located a bit lower; but still on the accessory case. (Lycoming engines, you may or may not have noticed, generally have a very "busy" accessory case, what with rear-mounted prop governors on the four-cylinder models, and hydraulic pump and fuel pump drives on the sixes.)

Hydraulic Versus Electric

Oil pressure gauges can be electric or hydraulic. In most aircraft, the gauging is hydraulic, with the oil pressure line terminating at a Bourdon-tube-type needle movement. (As pressure inside the clockspring-like Bourdon tube increases, the tube unfurls, moving the panel needle.) In some aircraft. like the Mooney 201, a pressure transducer is used to convert oil pressure—at the engine—to an electrical signal which can then be read by a volt/ohmmeter-type needle movement in the cockpit. The advantage of the latter system is obvious: In case of a plumbing fracture, hot oil is not released in the cockpit.

The disadvantage of the electric gauging system is that transducers fail more often than Bourdon tubes do, and poor electrical connections can give rise to false pressure readings. (In fact, a voltage regulator problem could give rise to a spuriously high or low oil pressure reading, in an aircraft like the Mooney 201.)

Questions of Interpretation

The question arises as to how literally the green arc (and redline) on the oil pressure gauge should be taken. There are times after all, when the oil is so thick on a cold morning that oil pressure goes into the red on takeoff. The answer is that the green arc is somewhat conservative (purposely); a Lycoming or Continental engine will operate safely, for considerable periods, with oil pressure outside the green—within reason.

Remember that the higher the power setting, the greater the lubrication demands of the engine, and the greater the oil pressure required to prevent damage. At 19-square (20 or 30 percent power), with hot oil, your engine doesn't need more than a few psi of oil pressure for safe operation—10 psi is plenty. But try to operate at 25-square (75- or 80-percent power) under 10-psi lubrication, and you're asking for trouble.

Oil pressure varies with viscosity. Inevitably, as cold oil becomes hot (and thins out), oil pressure drops. (Conversely, as oil cools and thickens, pressure will go up.)

Anything that thins your oil will give you a drop in oil pressure. That includes fuel dilution, the use of low-viscosity additives (such as

Marvel Mystery Oil and Microlon), and the mixing of winter-grade oil with summer-grade.

Although some pressure drop occurs upon heating with multigrade oils, Phillips X/C and Aeroshell Multigrade show less tendency toward heat-thinning than ordinary parafinnic oils. Conversely, multigrades show less tendency toward cold-congealing than straight-weights. If you want to guard against inflight prop dome and/or oil cooler congealing, use a multigrade.

Yet another factor in the oil-pressure equation is your prop governor. Next time you do your runup, watch what happens to oil pressure as you deep-cycle the prop. (In some planes, it goes down; in others, it goes up.) Knowledge of how your prop works is worth several psi in an oil-pressure emergency.

What do you do if you're flying along, and the oil pressure needle sags into the low green—maybe even *below* the low green? Check the oil temperature. If it's high, you should attempt to counteract heat-thinning of the oil by opening cowl flaps, reducing power, and (if possible) lowering the nose. (Back on the ground, remove your cowl and check for birds' nests and deteriorated cooling baffles.

If no obvious source of trouble can be found, pull and check the oil cooler thermostatic bypass valve. Also check the oil suction screen for signs of cavitation.)

If moderately low oil pressure—*unaccompanied* by high oil temperature—is noted in flight, don't panic: Reduce power as appropriate, and continue monitoring the pressure gauge. The key is to watch for "ticks" in the pressure. A sudden up-or down-tick of 5 to 20 psi almost surely indicates a piece of carbon hanging up on (or dislodging from) the oil pressure relief valve. (On most engines, this valve is located behind the right rear cylinder. Ask your mechanic to point it out.) This is easily correctable.

Maintenance Precautions

In rare cases, it may be necessary to "dial up" the engine's oil pressure by removing washers from (or turning the adjusting screw clockwise on) the pressure relief valve. (Most can be fiddled with.)

This is not something to be undertaken haphazardly, however. If chronic low oil pressure cannot be traced to high oil temperature, or to a damaged pressure relief valve seat, or dirt in the valve, consider the possibility that a leak has developed in a critical area (maybe in the gauge line itself). Perhaps a crankcase gallery has cracked internally (most likely to occur after a prop strike or other trauma).

Oil pressure gauges are almost troublefree, but you can foul things up when maintaining them by replacing the transducers with automotive-type P/Ns.

By the regulations, the orifices of any sensor on an aircraft are very small, to allow as much time as practicable before complete loss of fluids overboard, should one of the devices fail. Automotive-type pressure sensors are not subject to such constraints.

Many aircraft use an oil line from the engine to the oil pressure gauge; it pays to inspect carefully for leaks at the cockpit connection (gently tighten loose fittings—this, too, has an orifice).

On aircraft such as the J-3 Cub that have sat out in the winter without moving, it is often necessary to fill the oil line with a squirt can in order to obtain a pressure reading.

TACHOMETERS

Replacing a tachometer need not be a major source of trouble if you know well how the individual procedures tie into the whole operation. We will first look at the general procedures for mechanical and electric tachometers and then follow through with lessons from some hands-on experience.

Mechanical Tachometers

These are commonly mounted with Tinnerman type nutplates that will stay in place when you remove the mounting screws. Mechanical tachs are driven by a cable similar to that of an automobile's speedometer. Before you order a new tach or remove your original for overhaul, make sure the problem is not just with the tachometer drive cable. (Planes with long tach cables, and those with turbochargers to overheat everything, are particularly troublesome.)

Start by removing the knurled cable nut from the back of the tachometer with a pair of waterpump pliers. (When being reinstalled, it need not be much more than finger-tight.) Removing the cable from each tach usually requires a bit of wiggling and light pressure.

It's sometimes important to consider how you will put something back, at the instant you are removing it. Before reinstalling a tachometer in a panel, notice that the shaft's hole is broached square, to mate up with the square end of the drive cable. Don't attempt to force the cable in; rather, rotate it until it slips in. Also, make sure that the drive cable is not crimped or bent too sharply. It should be secured with tie-wraps every eight or ten inches, to preclude whipping. Drip some graphite speedometer lubricant into the drive cable before reinstalling

The engine end of the tach drive cable has a knurled attach nut. A little graphite speedo lube at this end helps ensure long cable life. It's also important to provide adequate support clamps to keep the cable from whipping around in flight.

After removing the mechanical tach, pry off its retaining ring.

it; but don't spill any on your upholstery, as it is nearly impossible to remove.

After the tachometer is reinstalled, take the slight amount of extra time to lubricate the other end of the drive cable, after removing its knurled knob at the engine accessory pad.

Most mechanical tachs are recording, using an odometer-type device to record the engine operating hours. Typically, they are made to be accurate only at a certain rpm (2,310 is common); this varies from aircraft model to aircraft model. (Be sure to specify the correct replacement P/N (and make a note of your old tach setting in the logs). Also, if you are replacing rather than overhauling a failed tach, have the instrument supplier adjust the hour meter—if possible—so that it matches the old instrument's reading. This costs only a few dollars and makes logbook entries a lot easier to decipher on subsequent annuals, title transfers, etc. Cheap tachs seem to run several hundred rpm off at deck angles other than level flight.

Electric Tachometers

Tach-generators, which supply an alternating current to indicators in the cockpit, are widely used on non-Piper twins to get away from long tach-cable runs that would be necessary with mechanical tachs. (No single-engine aircraft use electric tachometers.) The usual maintenance practice is to swap tach generators, fire up the aircraft, and see if the problem follows the generators. (Another favorite technique among mechanics—not necessarily recommended here—is to rev generator shafts with drill motors and observe cockpit indications.) The balance of the troubleshooting process is confined to checking wiring continuity, checking proper connections (it's easy to miswire tach-generators), and swapping out gauges and generators. Remove four screws and replace.

Tachometer Repair—Some Hands-on Lessons

It is one thing to describe the general procedure for even so simple an endeavor as replacing or repairing a tachometer; it is another thing to dive in with fingers and tools to do it. As we have before in this volume, we present here the actual experience of *Light Plane Maintenance* magazine contributing editor Michael L. Stockhill, as an educational service, to help you familiarize yourself with this equipment and its characteristics. (It bears repeating that Stockhill is an IA-rated A&P.) Here is how he described his tachometric adventure for *LPM:*
Happily, the process turned out to be fairly easy. Can you do it too? Probably. Can you do it legally? Not really, unless you have your work blessed by a duly authorized instrument repair facility. (Forget about an A&P signoff: No A&P can legally perform instrument repairs.)

Here, for anyone interested, is what I learned: Should you need to replace a tachometer and wish to keep the professional appearance of a silkscreened dialface, you can either have an instrument shop refinish the new tach's face to your specs, or you can swap your original dial face into a new tach. At the same time, the hourmeter can be adjusted.

I encourage you to start with the old tachometer, if you intend to do any of this, so you can get the process down pat without breaking anything expensive.

Disassembly

On AC tachs, and probably all off-brand varieties as well, the instrument glass (which is surrounded by a rubber seal roughly similar to an O-ring) is secured to the instrument case by means of a thin metal ring, which is crimped over a flange on the instrument case. The retaining ring must be removed by carefully prying along its perimeter with a suitable tool. (I used a simple blade screwdriver, although a similar implement with more rounded edges would better prevent damage to the retaining ring.) Work the crimped metal back along at least three quarters of the circumference and then pop the ring

Access comes by removing the gun-blued screws in the face of the instrument.

and glass off by prying through the gaps in the crimp at each of the mounting screw tabs.

Next, with a pair of needlenose pliers, remove the pointer to avoid damaging it. The tach's innards are freed by removing the two screws or bolts on the back of the instrument case, found on either side of the tachometer drive shaft. The dial face can be removed easily; just undo the two gun-blued screws on its face.

Before removing the hourmeter, which is a drumlike assembly with a stack of numeralled discs, look at the back side of the drum and note how the numbered discs are separated by small bright-metal rings with slotted fingers.

Note also that the row of slotted fingers is kept from turning by a metal blade. Before removing the drum, write down the old tach's indicated time. (If you wish, you can add that time to any other time from earlier tachs to get a total time in service for the aircraft.) Remove the recording hourmeter by holding the tachometer assembly so that it faces you as if installed in the aircraft. At the drum's left side there is a small clip that slips over the hourmeter shaft. Remove the clip (using either a screwdriver or needlenose pliers) and slide the hourmeter to the left until the right end of the shaft is free. Lift the hourmeter drum up and to the right until free.

Beating the Drum

My first impression as I tried to set the drum reminded me of my first confrontation with Rubik's cube. As I fumbled with the new instrument's hourmeter, it was only by sheer dumb luck that I dialed in the total time in service of my aircraft. Leaving well enough alone, I then toyed with the old hourmeter, confident that somehow it could be set systematically. In due time I stumbled upon the method, which turned out to be very easy. (I recommend that you experiment with the *old* hourmeter drum until you are ready to tackle the new tach.)

Start by holding the removed drum so you can read the numbers, with all of the slotted fingers lined up away from your face. When the hourmeter is installed in its cage, the displayed readout is exactly opposite the slotted fingers. Now. With your right-hand thumb and forefingers, hold the far *right* slotted finger so it cannot turn; then, with your left hand, rotate the balance of the drum's discs by working the small slotted fingers, keeping them all aligned. Each revolution will increase or decrease the displayed number by one digit, depending on which direction you go.

The total time in service of my Comanche was 2,501.83 hours. By turning the discs around in the foregoing manner three revolutions, the first digit set was the three. To set the eight (i.e., the second number from the right), I simply held two of the slotted fingers from turning with my right hand while rotating the rest of the discs with my left hand. The procedure is repeated for the remaining numbers, working right to left.

If that description seems confusing, be thankful you were not present during the discovery process. Suffice it to say, once the concept is grasped, it's easy enough for a fourth-grader.

Putting It Back

After you've played with your old hourmeter, by setting it to zero or something, practice reinstalling it in old tachometer mechanism. Using the reverse of the removal precedure, slip the left end of the shaft into the cage; align the slotted fingers and drop them over their metal retaining blade; then slip the right end of the shaft into place. Replace the retaining clip, and the unit is ready for reassembly.

Once you tire of experimenting and are reasonably satisfied that you won't break anything, you can tackle the new tach using the same methodology. Swap out the dial faces, as described; set the hourmeter;

The hour recording drum mechanism is deceptively simple in appearance.

and replace the pointer. The pointer is easily installed using needle-nose pliers. Be certain it is zeroed and that the needle is not bent so as to rub the dial or glass face. (Again, you may wish to practice on the old tach. The pointer is one item that could easily be broken if you aren't careful.) Finally, slip the assembly into the instrument case, reinstall the two case retaining screws, and reinstall the glass, seal, and retaining ring. (You will probably need to clean the glass before final installation.) I used a small ball-peen hammer to recrimp the retaining ring. Tap *lightly* and frequently, rather than smashingly.

After you're done, I encourage you to *keep your work legal by trotting over to your local instrument shop for a test run and the repairman's blessing.* Then the new tach, with its proper range marks and hourmeter setting, can be installed in your plane—with a logbook entry, from an A&P (yes, it's required).

Other than experience, what have you gained from all of this? You've saved a Jackson or two to have your dial face silkscreened to specs, plus ten bucks or so for setting the hourmeter. Presumably, you've bought a decent tachometer at a discount from a discount supplier rather than paying retail through your local Cessna or Piper dealer (if there still is such a thing). Perhaps you've also kept yourself from wasting a lot of time and aggravation on questionable alternatives to the name-brand-tach route. Tachs really are simple—once you get to know them.

EGT AND CHT

For many pilots, mixture management has become a matter for study; for others, a matter of deep concern; and for others, an obsession. They are all correct. The continuing high price of aviation fuel and a heightened awareness of the effects of lead buildup have led aircraft operators to adopt aggressive fuel-saving and damage preventive measures.

As a result, exhaust gas temperature and cylinder head temperature gauges have become vital to working airplanes. They are invaluable—but misconceptions about them can lead to confusion the equipment was purchased to avoid.

Common Myths About EGT

It's amazing how many pilots misunderstand the basics of EGT analysis. (Who can blame them? Most flight instructors don't understand it, either.) Probably the three most common EGT myths are:

1. The hottest cylinder and the leanest cylinder are the same.

2. The primary value of a multi-cylinder EGT system is in accurate mixture management.

3. Actual EGT numbers (in degrees Fahrenheit) are useful. (A corollary: The more accurate the EGT gauge, the better.)

In case you missed the first semester of Combustion Chemistry 101, your engine's leanest cylinder, by definition, is *the cylinder that reaches peak EGT first, when the mixture control is pulled back.* This may or not be the hottest cylinder. (If you think about it, there is no reason to expect that the leanest cylinder *should* be the hottest, since the actual value of peak EGT can be high or low, depending on cylinder compression that day.) Your leanest cylinder may be the one that gets the most air. Or it can be the jug that gets the least fuel. Or both. Moreover, the leanest cylinder *can change from day to day,* as rings shift, valves seat differently, etc. A plugged injector nozzle will make *any* cylinder suddenly the "leanest cylinder."

Having four or six EGT probes instead of one isn't going to make you lean your engine four or six times more accurately, so banish the thought that you're buying an exhaust analyzer for mixture-management purposes. The main reason anyone upgrades from a single-

The single-probe exhaust gas tempera-ture gauge was revolutionary in its time, but has been surpassed by the multi-probe EGT as well as instruments that combine cylinder head tempera-tures (CHT) and turbine inlet tempera-tures (TIT)—in turbocharged aircraft—to analyze engine health and trends.

probe system to a multi-probe system is to exploit the EGT's *trouble-shooting capabilities.* This doesn't just mean being able to pinpoint a problem jug after it's dead. In the hands of a knowledgeable operator, a multi-probe EGT can actually be used to *anticipate* trouble—to *see into the future.* As a side benefit you'll be able to tell your mechanic which cylinder to look at, and why.

If you're one of the many wing nuts who thinks raw EGT numbers are important, think again. Except in TIT-limited engines, *actual exhaust temperatures are of no practical consequence whatsoever.* After all, what does an EGT reading of, say, 1,437° Fahrenheit tell you? Unless you refer it to something else, *it doesn't tell you anything.* Just knowing that the EGT is 1,437 doesn't tell you whether you're on the rich side of peak, or on the lean side, for example. It certainly doesn't tell you if both magnetos are on line (or whether mag timing is drifting early); or if one or the other spark splug is fouled; or whether an induction air leak has developed; or if the cylinder is detonating; or if an injector nozzle is clogging up. (It certainly doesn't tell you if you're looking at the richest jug, or the leanest one.)

For The Upgrader, an Explosion of Choices

Buying a wristwatch used to be a simple thing. You could get big numbers, or small ones (glow-in-the-dark, optional), with a calendar window on really fancy models. But now it's a whole different story: Just getting *hands* instead of liquid-crystal digits is a major feat, and if you don't want a timepiece that calculates the perihelion of Mercury while beeping to remind you that your systolic blood pressure is low, you've got darn little to choose from.

A similar revolution has been taking place in EGTs. Where once all exhaust gas gauge temperature gauges were of the Mickey Mouse (analog) single-needle type, now the aircraft owner can choose from a bafflingly diverse array of setups, including:

1. Multiple-probe, single-needle analog EGT, switchable. (Alcor "Exhaust Analyzer.")

2. Multiple-probe, multiple-needle analog EGT. (Alcor, KS Avionics.)

3. Multiple-probe EGT & CHT, analog display, switchable by mode and by cylinder. (KS Avionics.)

4. Single-probe EGT, single-probe CHT, plus oil temperature, LCD display, switchable by mode. (Electronics International.)

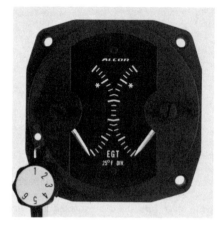

Alcor's 12-probe unit for twins.

5. Single-probe liquid-crystal digital EGT. (Electronics International.)

6. Single-probe LCD-type EGT and CHT, switchable by mode. (Electronics International.)

7. Multiple-probe LCD-type EGT, switchable by cylinder. (Electronics Intl., KS Avionics.)

8. Multiple-probe LCD-type CHT, switchable by cylinder. (Electronics Intl., KS Avionics.)

9. Multiengine version of the above, switchable by engine. (Electronics Intl.)

10. Multiple-probe EGT/CHT (with TIT), plasma-dicharge bar-graph display. (Insight GEM.)

The key question facing the owner who wants to upgrade is: Which of these systems is best, not only from the standpoint of efficient utilization of panel space and most-features-for-dollars-spent, but

Switchables

The cheapest and easiest way to upgrade an EGT, of course, is to add more probes and put a selector switch on the panel, giving your existing single-needle (or single-LCD) panel gauge multichannel capability. And despite the current trend towards high-tech "all in

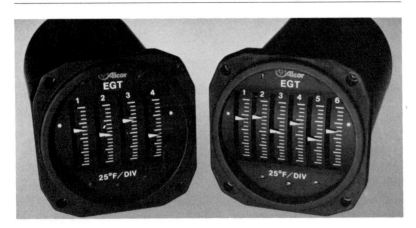

The multi-probe display that allows simultaneous readings on all the cylinders is a major advance. It permits the pilot to view trends, not just spot-check today's leanest or hottest cylinder.

one" multi-needle display systems (Such as the new Alcor and Insight GEM gauges), switchable systems continue to be popular, simply because they *are* cheap and easy to install, while making good use of panel space.

But there are serious drawbacks. Adding a selector knob does give you access to more engine information—but you're ignoring most of it, most of the time. (In a four-cylinder engine, you're ignoring 75 percent of your cylinders 100 percent of the time. In a six-banger you're ignoring 83 percent of your cylinders 100 percent of the time.)

To cross-check cylinders with a switchable EGT requires not only an excellent short-term memory but a spare hand or hands to flip the switch and lean the mixture. Also, finding the leanest cylinder (as opposed to the hottest cylinder) takes time, and once the mixture has been set, inflight trend monitoring to detect signs of trouble is difficult unless you sit there and fiddle constantly with the selector knob.

The term "exhaust analyzer," as applied to switchable systems, is a misnomer. Such systems actually analyze nothing. It's the *pilot* who analyzes, playing cylinder roulette (flipping by selector), memorizing numbers, determining temperature trends across time, and coming up with a coherent picture of the engine's operational status (all while performing a normal IFR scan, of course, and talking to ATC). Trouble-shooting becomes an after-the -fact exercise: Once a cylinder is dead (or dying), you can isolate it quickly. But as for spotting intermittent problems, you just have to hope the glitch occurs on the

Athough a digital EGT display offers great precision, at times the precision is unnecessary and misleading.

jug that happens to be selected at the moment; if it occurs on a non-selected cylinder, you'll never see it. Because it is a hassel to switch switches and perform mental arithmetic all the time, many owners of switchable EGTs make it a practice simply to leave the selector knob on the "leanest cylinder" from flight to flight, rotating the dial only when trouble is suspected. There are two problems with this. first, the leanest cylinder can change at any time. (A plugged injector nozzle is all it takes.) Second, the lack of ability to see inter-cylinder EGT *trends* makes it impossible to spot developing engine problems *before* they become major—which is one of the main reasons to have a multichannel EGT in the first place.

Trend Monitoring

The long and the short of it is: To use an EGT system to maximum advantage, you have to be able to discern *trends*. Most leaning is done by reference to peak EGT on the leanest cylinder, for example, and the leanest cylinder *can only be found by trend information*. (The actual numeric value of peak EGT—in degrees Fahrenheit—on the leanest cylinder is of no significance. As we have seen, the leanest cylinder and hottest cylinder aren't necessarily the same. (trend monitoring is also the key to engine troubleshooting. Only by noting *changes* in intercylinder EGT patterns can the pilot get an early warning of impending trouble, be it minor (e.g., plug fouling, injector nozzle

The Graphic Engine Monitor allows full-time, all-cylinder display of EGT, CHT and even TIT, if applicable.

gumming) or major (ring breakage, valve sticking). There's no way a pilot can get a jump on trouble (see into the future) if he or she can't *spot and track* temperature variations *as they're occurring.* Once a failure has occured, of course, a switchable system will allow the pilot to isolate the failure to the affected cylinder— which is more than the owner of a single-probe system can do. But the ability to point to a broken cylinder after it breaks is nowhere near as valuable as the ability to spot trouble *before it happens* (or at least, before it becomes a threat to airworthiness).

Digital vs. Analog

If you like Japanese wristwatches, you've probably been intrigued by the appearance of liquid-crystal display (LCD) type of EGT gauges. These gauges have been available for about six years from Electronics International (and more recently, KS Avionics). And certainly, if one-degree accuracy were essential to leaning an aircraft engine, a digital readout would be tremendously beneficial. As it turns out, of course, one-degree accuracy is *not* necessary (or even desirable) in an EGT system. A one-degree change in EGT is simply never of practical importance to the pilot—or the engine.

Imagine for a minute the wall-of numbers effect that would result if all cockpit indications—not just EGT and CHT, but airspeed, altitude, rate of climb, heading, VOR bearing, ammeter load, etc.—were displayed in digital (i.e., numeric) form. The pilot could never assimilate the data; it would be a nightmare of information overload. (Actually, the *amount* of information hasn't changed—only the presentation. Which illustrates an important point: How you display information in a cockpit *does matter.* Ergonomics is no joke, even at the level of a VFR general-aviation panel, let alone F-16s and 757s.)

Perhaps it's not surprising, then, that no one has yet come out with a simultaneous, all-cylinder display of EGT in liquid-crystal numerals. All multicylinder EGTs that use a straight numeric presentation tend to be of the switchable

A look at the GEM circuit board shows the parts count is low, placing the major importance on software features.

variety—with all the drawbacks (in terms of high pilot workload, difficulty of trend monitoring, etc.) that that entails.

The bottom line? A straight numeric presentation makes sense for such things as outside air temperature (which tends to be static) or fuel quantity (where extreme accuracy is important), or even cylinder head temperature (for which there are definite go/no-go limits). But for something as dynamic as EGT monitoring—where the individual numbers change often (and mean nothing out of context)—an analog approach seem more appropriate.

Of course, if you *don't mind* switching back and forth between cylinders in flight, constantly comparing numbers and mentally calculating intercylinder EGT spreads (as well as EGT *trends* over time) to arrive at a determination of the leanest cylinder versus richest—to say nothing of trouble-shooting plugged injector nozzles, drifting mag timing, and/or other problems, while watching the numbers flicker as you climb or descend—upgrading to a switchable LCD-type EGT may well be cost-effective for you.

It isn't for us.

Scanners

Pilot workload in a high-performance aircraft is sufficiently high (in an IFR environment especially) that the introduction of yet another switchable gauge in the cockpit, when nonswitchable alternatives are available, doesn't make good sense from a safety point of view (never mind engine diagnostics). One manufacturer, recognizing this, has come up with a "channel scanning" feature (not unlike the scanners used on police band radios) to allow the pilot to see all cylinders' EGT readouts *in sequence*, automatically, without the need for removing one hand from the controls.

J.P. Instruments of Huntington Beach, California offers scanning-type EGT/CHT (with both EGT and CHT combined into one 2.25-inch panel display), starting at $789 for a 4-cylinder EGT-only system, and going to $1,395 for a 6-cylinder combined EGT/CHT system (including probes). Seven-, 8-, and 9-cylinder models are available on request.

The instrument sold by J.P. has a manual mode in which the pilot can linger on one cylinder or step through the cylinders by pushing a button, as well as an "automatic" mode in which the LED-type display flashes the EGT (or CHT) for each cylinder in sequence, at the rate of four to five seconds per cylinder readout. (In other words, it takes 30 seconds or so to cycle through all six EGT readouts for an IO-520)

The J.P. Scanner represents a step in the right direction. But the problem of information assimilation remains. How can a busy pilot *absorb and remember* EGT trend data as an instrument flashes sequences of numbers corresponding to exhaust gas temperature for individual cylinders? How can long-term trends be discerned?

More to the point: How can the leanest cylinder be found with such a device? (J.P. Instruments' literature states that "normal leaning is accomplished on the hottest cylinder in the Manual mode," but makes no reference to the *leanest* cylinder—which is something entirely different.)

How a busy IFR pilot would fit the J.P. scanner's nominal 30-second duty cycle into a normal IFR panel scan is not immediately obvious, either, but assuming it can be done, the question arises whether the scanning feature makes troubleshooting any easier (except in the case of a totally dead jug). It is still up to the pilot to monitor cylinders, mentally calculate EGT spreads, observe trends, and formulate a coherent mental picture of engine health.

The J.P. Instrument Scanner is arguably one notch better than a manually switchable EGT (and many pilots will prefer the bright LED-type readout to a passively lit liquid-crystal display). But from a troubleshooting standpoint—or even for finding an engine's leanest cylinder—the device's value is moot-squared, multiplied by four (or six, as appropriate).

All-Cylinder Displays: Analog

The ergonomic shortcomings of the "switchable digitals" are largely overcome in the analog-meter all-cylinder EGTs manufactured by Alcor and KS Avionics. Alcor's vertical readout multineedle gauges indicate EGT only (switchable by engine, for twins) and start at $2,063.95 for a six cylinder kit. KS Avionics' vertical readout gauges indicate EGT *or* EGT/CHT (switchable by mode) and can be ordered with overtemp annunciation. KSA's Hexad six-cylinder EGT with overtemp alarms for each cylinder lists at $1,174 ($1,475 with CHT). Alcor's gauge is EGT-only.

Neither the Alcor nor the KSA vertical read-out gauges come with numbered scales. (Scale divisions, however, are 25° Fahrenheit per hash mark in each case.) The lowest indication on the Alcor instrument corresponds to about 1,300 degrees; hence, no reading at idle (and none at runup, for most aircraft). KSA's gauges, on the other hand, have an expandable scale: By adjusting tiny control knobs at the bottoms of the meters, the gauge's pointers can be made to indicate across a range from 900 to 1,800°F, making runup diagnostics a cinch.

For this study, we flew a normally aspirated Piper Seminole with the Alcor multineedle gauge, switchable by engine. In a nutshell, the Alcor instrument (which we assume was properly calibrated) did everything we would expect a non-annunciating all-cylinder EGT to do, except provide useful indications during the mag check. (Two needles came off their pegs, barely, during runup.) Response time was quick, and the display was easy to read, permitting a rapid assessment of intercylinder EGT spreads at a glance. For an EGT-only type gauge, the Alcor unit gets high marks. (Alcor does make a twin-engine "flip-flop," but no EGT/CHT switchables; and none of Alcor's gauges has warning lights.)

KSA's Tetra and Hexad (4-and 6-cylinder) EGT/CHT systems operate in similar fashion to Alcor's multi-display heads, with a few important differences. One difference is, CHT can be displayed on the same gauge at the flick of a mode switch (not possible with the Alcor unit). Secondly, various types of annunciation are available on KSA's gauges, including EGT overtemp (by cylinder), TIT overtemp, CHT overtemp, and CHT shock cooling.

Probably the biggest difference between KSA's vertical-readout EGTs and Alcor's is the pointer-alignment feature. At the bottom of each meter is an adjustment dial, the purpose of which is to allow the pilot to set the indicator needle to any height desired. According to KSA, this allows the pilot to do two worthwhile things, one being to expand the useful range of the instrument (which has a normal 250° peg-to-peg scale), and the other being to let the pilot line up all pointers in cruise (after final leaning) so that any EGT excursions are immediately apparent.

At first blush, the notion of being able to "zero out" one's normal EGT spread (so as to facilitate future troubleshooting) sounds eminently reasonable. But—leaving aside questions about calibration error— we think it's good to be able to see the day-today pattern of peaks and dips in EGTs between cylinders. We *want* to be able to see EGT spread on each flight. We *want* to know that, hey, cylinder number two is running awfully damn hot today compared to cylinder number one, in relation to yesterday's flight; wonder if induction air leak is developing? (Wonder if a spark plug is crapping out?) If you keep zeroing out the pointers, you may just lose sight of what's normal, and what's not, for the various cylinders. You might even zero out a bonafide problem.

Of course, it is cute to be able to lean the engine *almost* to peak, then quickly zero out the needle (lining them up in a neat row), then continue leaning until one pointer suddenly drops—revealing (presto!) the leanest jug.

But unfortunately, once you zero out the pointers in flight, you can't readily un-zero them—you can't look at your normal intercylinder spread again, unless you happen to remember which way all the needle-adjustment knobs were pointing before you turned them. (A niggling complaint, but there you are.)

Because of the adjustment knobs, the clear plastic covers over the meters, and the unusual scale markings on its gauges, KSA's Tetra and Hexad display have a cluttered look compared to Alcor's vertical-needle EGTs. But by the same token, KSA's gauges display more information (CHT as well as EGt) and provide more features than the Alcor units. After looking at both, we only wish an Alcor gauge were available that could switch back and forth between EGT and CHT.

All-Cylinder Displays: Digital

The other Prime Contender in the all-cylinder vertical-readout EGT-CHT arena—and certainly in a class by itself for display design—is the Graphic Engine Monitor, made by Insight Instrument Corporation. Probably no other engine instrument appearing in the last decade has had as profound an effect on the market as the GEM (which is singlehandedly responsible for the recent trend towards all-cylinder EGT displays). Also, no other instrument is as widely misunderstood.

The GEM displays EGT, CHT and TIT (turbine inlet temperature) information all at once (continuously), on the same 2.25-inch panel display, and is the only instrument on the market to do so. (Others flip-flop between modes.) EGT is displayed as one column per cylinder, and one bar for each 25°. CHT is displayed as a *non-illuminated* (dark) bar in each stack of orange bars. TIT (if applicable) is depicted as a numeric readout at the top of the gauge. An expanded scale allows the GEM to read out EGT at temperatures as low as 800° making runup diagnostics possible. CHT indications are referenced to an absolute scale (200-500°) represented by the numbers 2, 3, and 4 arranged vertically along the right edge of the gauge.

Also for this study, we flew a normally aspirated 1977 Piper Lance, equipped with a Model 602 Graphic Engine Monitor wired for EGT and CHT. As advertised, the unit's display began "stacking bars" only seconds after engine start, with CHT clearly readable by the time we pulled out of the tie-down spot. During the mag check, we were able to monitor the EGT rise on single-mag operation. A check of the mixture control showed it was possible to get a large (five or six-bar) rise in EGT even at as little as 1,700 rpm.

In flight, the GEM has two modes of operation. The *lean mode* is selected by pushing the tiny mode button and holding it in for about two seconds, which makes the orange "EGT" letters start flashing in the upper left portion of the display. At this point, you can begin coming back on the mixture lever (the EGT bar-stacks will rise accordingly); meanwhile, the GEM's microprocessor—which is tracking the EGT rise for each cylinder as a function of time (and *comparing* cylinders with each other)—determines which of your cylinders is leanest *and begins flashing the appropriate stack of bars* as that cylinder approaches peak. (On our Lance, it was cylinder number three.)

When the leanest cylinder's readout starts flashing, you can punch the mode button to stop the flashing (thus entering the *monitor mode*) and either keep the mixture control where it is —i.e., at peak EGT on the leanest cylinder—or enrichen as desired for cruise.

In the monitor mode, the GEM displays realtime EGTs continuously and monitors all cylinders for temperature excursions. If any EGT readout increases by more than 50°, that cylinder's bar-stack will begin flashing (and *keep on* flashing until the pilot hits the reset button). Intermittent problems, such as a fouling spark plug, are thus revealed in clear fashion so that even if the pilot is busy in the cockpit and doesn't happen to be looking at the EGT when the problem happens, he or she can still know about it.

Critics of the GEM carp about its supposedly coarse 25° resolution, noting that a 10° change in EGT (or CHT) can go undisplayed.

But as it turns out, the GEM's computer brain actually senses and tracks EGT with fraction-of a-degree accuracy; the *panel display* resolution merely happens to be 25°.

Insight Instrument Corporation's John Youngquist (designer of the GEM) flight-tested several versions of the GEM in his Bonanza before arriving at the final display configuration.

"The GEM's 25° resolution is no accident," Youngquist is quick to point out. "The first GEM prototype was a10° per-bar device—and it was terrible. The bars were floating all over the place. Normal everyday temperature changes were too distracting at that resolution.

"So we updated the softwear and tried 'tuning' the resolution. We experimented and found that 25° resolution was actually best from the standpoint of being easy to read without being distracting or sending a lot of 'false alarms' to the pilot.

"You know, you have to ask yourself what it is you want the gauge to display. And we asked that question. We actually started from a clean sheet of paper, asking 'What do we want this thing to show?' And we came up with what we have now."

We happen to agree with Youngquist, in any case. A display accuracy of one part in two thousand (easily possible with an LCD-type readout) is not really appropriate to EGT analysis as practiced by the majority of pilots. After all, when most leaning is done to an arbitrarily chosen setpoint of 50° or 75°, (or 100, or 125) degrees rich of peak, why worry about whether you've accidently gone to 51° degrees or 76°.

Likewise, it is hard to imagine a troubleshooting situation in which 1° (or even 10°) accuracy would be paramount.

Considering the GEM's ease of use/interpretation, its annunciation features, and its ability to display CHT, EGT, and TIT all at once (to say nothing of the device's space-age charisma), the list price of $1,732 for the six-cylinder GEM (including probes) strikes us as not unreasonable—downright attractive, even.

If only it would calculate the perihelion of Mercury and give a readout of systolic blood pressure ...

CHT (and Oil Temperature) Readings:
A Warning About Warnings

There is nothing quite like the dampening sense of unease that can beset a pilot when his scanning eyes pick up high cylinder head or oil temperature indications. Visions ranging from a disintergrating to a merely delay-causing engine immediately assault his serenity and can needlessly nick his wallet.

Lycoming factory officials state that from time to time, they receive queries from operators regarding the cause(s) and cure(s) of high oil and cylinder head temperatures. They also state that in many cases, it is "not an engine problem causing the high reading, but the oil or cylinder head instrument or systems giving false readings."

The moral is obvious: If you have a high oil temp or CHT problem, check the simple things first. I.e., inspect your oil temp and CHT gauge

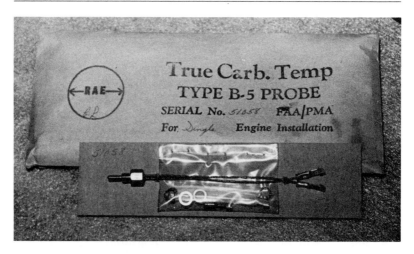

The Richter B-5 carb temp sender is approved for most carburetors.

connections, senders, routings, etc. *first* ... then investigate the potentially more expensive possibilities. What appears to be a serious overheating problem may, in reality, be a simple malfunction of a $10 probe or sender.

CHT/Plus Carb Temp Gauge:
Impressive Side Benefits

In converting a 180-hp Piper Comanche to turbocharging, an *LPM* editor determined that he would first want to have in his panel not only a CHT but a carburetor temperature gauge (as much for limiting inlet temperatures as for monitoring the possible buildup of a carburetor or induction icing). He purchased a Richter B-5 combination carb temp and CHT indicating system, which he elected to install himself. What the installation entailed will be described shortly, but first, it is instructive to see just what the benefits of a carb temp indicator are. The manufacturer's description of those advantages have proved to be reasonable:

"A major spark plug manufacturer has found that lead deposits on the plugs in engines using higher octane gasoline are usually the result of inadequate volatilization of the antiknock compounds used to raise the octane rating of the fuel. Most such fuels contain tetraethyl lead, which if allowed to burn without an inhibitor, would form metallic lead oxide. Therefore another substance, ethylene dibromide, is added to the fuel along with the tetraethyl lead. The (resulting)

The Richter B-5 probe goes into a pre-existing hole in a typical Marvel Schebler (Facet) MA-4-5.

combustion product is lead bromide, a fine powder which is readily blown out the exhaust system. But gasoline has a lower vaporization temperature than ethylene dibromide, which in turn vaporizes more easily than tetraethyl lead. So if the mixture is too cold in the carburetor to vaporize all the fuel components properly, the tetraethyl lead may be concentrated in only a part of the engine, in the form of large, heavy droplets, and possibly separated from its inhibiting ethylene dibromide. During combustion, therefore, lead oxide may be formed. This lands on the lowest point in the cylinder, the lower spark plugs, which then foul out. To avoid this, *it has been found that warming the fuel-air mixture in the carburetor will aid the volatilization of all the fuel elements together.*

"Experiments have shown that an indicated temperature of about 5° Celsius above freezing measured at the throttle valve will assure proper volatilization, *increasing plug life and engine reliability.* Leaning the mixture to compensate for the slight richening due to heated carburetor air should result in fuel economy equal to or even better than that experienced when fuel is mixed with very cold air. This applies to cruise power conditions. For maximum power, the densest available, hence coldest, air is required."

CHT/Carb Temp Gauge Installation:
Tools and Materials

The tool list for this job is pretty basic. You'll need screwdrivers, a set of socket wrenches, and terminal connector pliers. In the event that your carburetor is a real oldie, it may be necessary to have the temperature probe's mount hole drilled out and tapped for a 1/4-by-28 thread.

The gauge and probes are normally available in a kit (manufactured by Aircraft Instrument & Development, Inc., R.C. Allen Instrument Division) that includes the meter, an AN5546-1 resistance probe for measuring cylinder head temperature, the aforementioned Richter B-5 resistance probe to measure carburetor throat temperature, and a clunky old MS31006A-14S—5S connector receptacle. For those unable

The MS3106A-14S-5S connector is shown after wires have been soldered in place and shrink-fit tubing put on.

to get a trade discount, the kit is available (under P/N 71-509-4) from Aircraft Components, Inc. (ACI, P.O. Box 1188, Benton Harbor, MI 49022). These kits are ideal, by the way, for those whose aircraft either do not have a cylinder head temperature gauge (or a CHT that's the large 3-1/8-inch style). Those with an extra 2-1/4-inch hole in their panel can order a small gauge with the B-5 probe for carb temp only from ACI (P/N 71-340-4). Additional alternatives include digital combination outside air temperature and carburetor temp gauges, and even ARP carb ice detectors (which use an optical probe instead of the B-5's temperature bulb). Completion of any of these installations is basically the same.

These gauge systems are generally approved for all Marvel-Schebler and Bendix-Stromberg carburetors, although certain engine series do not have specific STCs. Ironically this owner's Lycoming O-360-AIA was excluded from the Richter probe's STC list, although the list shows approvals for all other O-360s except the C2B and C2D; so it was necessary for him to obtain a field approval from the local FAA GADO office.

Panel Mounting

The project was begun by physically mounting the gauge in the panel, after removing the old cylinder head temperature gauge, using the procedure discussed in Chapter 1. (As the gauge is only about 2.6 inches deep, clearance should pose no problem.)

Next, a power source was selected, for the instrument does require bus power. For the benefit of anyone who comes upon the gauge separately, the instrument can be wired to its terminal A for 28 volts, and to terminal D for 14 volts. Terminal B goes to the cylinder temperature bulb, terminal E to the B-5 carb temp sensor, and terminal C is the common ground (on negative-ground systems) for the gauge and both temperature probes. As he flies IFR on occasion he does not indiscriminately wire incidental ancillaries to circuits such as avion-

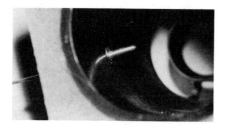

Probe in carb throat: depth is critical.

ics, turn coordinators, panel lights, pitot heat, ar any other device he would hate to lose if a gauge with no on/off switch had a direct short. Ultimately, he settled on the fuel gauge circuit, and planned a lead long enough to reach its circuit breaker. In many planes, the fuel gauges do not have a "dedicated" CB but share a breaker with other accessories. Check your plane's wiring diagram carefully before proceeding.

Since a couple of the leads necessarily go forward of the firewall, shielded wire was used, for increased abrasion resistance. The wiring harness was built up by disassembling the MS3106-14S-5S connector, pretinning its terminals, and soldering the four wires in place. Be sure to color code or otherwise mark the wires, so you know which wire goes to each of the terminals. The wires in this case were cut to substantially varying lengths, and were thus kept track of using length as a code (the longest wire, obviously, went to the carburetor, farthest away from the gauge.) Finally, the wiring harness was protected from abrasion by using a short piece of shrink-fit tubing over the end of the fitting.

Under the Hood

Moving on up to the engine compartment, the old gasket-style thermocouple was removed from the right rear cylinder (by removing the spark plug, fishing out the thermocouple, and reinstalling the plug with a fresh copper gasket).

In the bottom of the cylinder head, an AN4076-1 adaptor fitting was installed. It simply screws into the prethreaded hole that already exists there; then the bayonet-style cylinder head temperature probe was plugged into place.

The carburetor temperature bulb was another matter. With more contemporary carburetors (probably those built after the mid-sixties), the hole for this probe is factory-tapped, and merely requires unscrewing the existing threaded plug and screwing the probe into the hole, using a single shakeproof washer as the means of safetying. In this case, however, it was necessary to remove the carburetor, and remove a lead plug from the hole, which was step-drilled. The installation instructions suggest drilling out the lead plug with a 7/32 inch drill, and they require counterboring a flat on the boss.

These latter chores were completed easily, then the hole was tapped with a 1/4-by 28 thread tap. The installation requires some dabbling around to adjust the temperature probe so that it doesn't protrude too far into the carburetor throat. The instructions are thorough, though, on this matter, and the probe manufacturer is insistent in the description of which—and how many—shim washers can be used. As the carburetor casting is very expensive, it pays to have a machine shop do the facing and threading work, unless you have undying faith in the craftsmanship of your local A&P. (Since he had the carburetor removed from the plane, with metal chips flying about—and since the carb was quite old to begin with—the owner elected to diassemble the unit completely and overhaul it at the same time.)

Final Hookup

At this point, the wiring harness was connected to the gauge, and the FWF (firewall-forward) leads were run through a convenient grommet, then run through a vinyl tube for abrasion resistance and connected to the two probes.

Remember that electrical leads must always be routed above, not below, fluid and fuel lines. A common airframe ground was used for both probes, with separate wiring.

Finally, tie-wrap the cable and leads at convenient lengths for vibration (and chafe) control, do a functional test, and—if you want to stay legal—have a mechanic inspect and sign off your work as a minor alteration, referring (in the logbook entry) to the Richter temperature probe's STC. If your particular engine doesn't appear on the STC list, have an IA-rated A&P run the necessary paperwork through on an FAA Form 337 for a field approval, which should be granted with no difficulty.

Even including the time spent removing the cowl, making the wiring harness, and removing the carburetor, the project consumed less than five hours.

From powerplant telltales we'll now proceed to what is perhaps an even more exotic area—electronics— in which, as we shall see, keeping one's radios alive is only one of many maintenance opportunities.

Part II
ELECTRICAL EQUIPMENT

Chapter 4

UNDER
THE WIRE

Today's airplanes, however large, however small, are airborne nervous systems. In our time, only the most basic (primitive?) VFR flying is independent of boxes, connections, and other parts that look, listen, report, and point the way, if not to the future, at least to the next waypoint. Any IFR sortie is composed of one nervous system (the pilot) working in close partnership with another, electro-mechanical, one. And if one or the other—or both—of the systems fails, the workload on the remaining devices and the crew is bound to increase rapidly and exponentially.

If electronic devices fail in flight, there are emergency procedures that can help the pilot to retain a good chance of at least getting down safely and quite possibly completing the flight at the intended destination. However, these are only stopgap measures which, in the worst circumstances, are not guaranteed to save the situation. And while most of the devices—from radios to lighting systems—perform with relatively good reliability over the short term, the long-term prospects for any piece of equipment can be open to doubt.

Proper maintenance can help to lengthen their life. This chapter will offer tips on practices for protecting some electronic devices from aerial breakdowns.

SURVIVAL TIPS FOR OLD RADIOS

If one thing is certain in the uncertain world of lightplane electronics, it's that today's technological breakthrough is tomorrow's museum piece. What's frightening about this is that the entire journey from showroom shelf to garbage pail can take less than ten years, for some radios—and the useful half-life of our black boxes does not appear to be getting any longer. In fact, it may be getting shorter.

A variety of factors is conspiring to render all of today's radios worthless junk in the next ten years. Poor quality control is one factor; no radio with a mean time between failures (MTBF) of less than 600 hours—and there are plenty of them around—is going to make it to the mid-1990s with out extraordinary life-preserving measures. (And even if such a radio *did* survive the coming decade, it would have zero salvage value.) Beyond that is the problem of design obsolescence and unrepairability; replacement parts will not be available in ten years for most of the radios now flying. And if the parts *were* available, you wouldn't want to pay the price.

Another thing to consider—and this is something almost nobody these days is thinking about—is that natural economic forces will compel the smaller avionics producers to become highly specialized or drop out of the market. The situation that exists today with regard to avionics is not unlike the scenario that prevailed with the airframe manufacturers after World War II; a profusion of manufacturers and products exists for which there is no sustainable market. Only the titans of the industry will survive.

In other words, you may not have a parts backup for your black boxes five or ten years from now. Chances are that your particular radios will be extinct by then.

All of which points to the necessity of keeping your present radios in top shape and getting on good terms with your local avionics technician. From a preventive maintenance standpoint, there are several things you can do—beginning today—to keep your black boxes healthy.

Moisture and Heat

Water does bad things to radios. In addition to causing out-and-out short circuits, moisture can corrode relay and switch contacts and deteriorate insulation. (A few drops of standing water can—over time—thoroughly wreck a poorly sealed RF or IF transformer.) To avoid water-related problems, it is necessary to trace cockpit leaks to their source and fix them. (Windshield leaks—perhaps the most common source of entry of water into the instrument panel—can be eliminated through the judicious use of 3M Strip Calk. You can buy Strip Calk at most any hardware store.)

If your plane is stored in a particularly humid area, you might consider placing bags of desiccant in and around the instrument panel between flights. Heat, like water, has an extremely deleterious effect on electronic equipment—and here again, airplane cockpits can be somewhat less than hospitable environments. On a warm (85°F) day, passive solar heating can raise the cockpit temperature of a parked aircraft to *160°F (71°C) or more.* By comparison, TSO requirements for many types of avionics call for continuous-operation to be demonstrated at 160°F. (Some deterioration of power-transistor performance can be observed, typically, at temperatures as low as 77°F/25°C; failure occurs at approximately 257°F/125°C.)

What this means, very simply, is that when you climb into your cockpit on a hot day and turn on all your radios, you are operating them in an environment that *exceeds* TSO requirements for high-temperature reliability. It is not an environment conducive to long radio life.

Several things can be done to protect your avionics from the ravages of heat. The first (and most important) thing you can do is install a windshield sunscreen, assuming the aircraft is not routinely hangared. (Even if it *is* routinely hangared, you should carry a sunscreen for those occasions when the plane may have to be tied down outside at strange airports.)

A good suncreen will keep cabin air temperatures within a few degrees of the outside air temperature at all times, thereby prolonging not only radio life, but instrument and upholstery life as well. (Custom-made sunscreens are available through a variety of sources, or you can fabricate your own screen using heat reflective "space blanket" material obtained through a local harware or department store.)

Something else you can do to minimize the risk of heat damage to your black boxes is keep them turned off until you need to use them. Due to the way radios are often stacked, adjacent radios tend to absorb each other's heat. (Since heated air rises, the number-one navcom—top dog in the pile—generally suffers the most in this regard and is often the first unit in the stack to fail.)

This being the case, it only makes sense to turn on but *one* com set—plus, say, the transponder—and keep all other boxes *off* until cruising altitude (i.e., cool air) is reached.

Air conditioning, of course, can be expected to lessen the likelihood of heat damage—but only if (again) the radios in a warm cabin are left *off* long enough for the air conditioning to begin to be felt. Allow five to ten minutes after the start of air conditioning for the black boxes to become cold-soaked before flipping the swiches on.

If you don't have or don't want to spend the money necessary to install air conditioning, you may well want to consider installing an inexpensive electric fan behind the panel, to circulate cooling air

In most cases, removing a radio from its tray requires only loosening a couple of screws at the front. Then a healthy tug allows the box to slide out. This vintage ARC navcom has retaining screws at the top corners. Remember to loosen them only enough to remove the radio, not to allow the screws to fall out and get lost.

around the radio trays. Any avionics shop can handle the installation job, if your mechanic can't do it or doesn't want to sign off your work.

Pre-Digital-Age Avionics

From a preventive maintenance standpoint, keeping radios *cool* and *dry* is without question the most important thing you can do to enhance avionics reliability. If you own relatively new equipment (i.e., solid-state, modular, lightweight equipment), keeping radios cool and dry may be the *only* things you can legally do to increase avionics reliability, aside from turning radios off prior to engine startup (to guard against voltage-spike damage).

On the other hand, if your equipment is of the pre-digital-era, hard-wired, tube-studded variety (a surprising amount of radios still are), there are a couple more things you can do to extend radio life.

After a tube-equipped radio (and that means not only older navcoms, but more recent transponders and DMEs, too) has been in service ten years or more, you can expect some of those tubes to start becoming a bit senile. Unlike solid-state components, tubes *wear out* as they are used, the exact extent of the wear depending on how severely the tubes are stressed by the given circuit(s).

Different tubes have different life expectancies. Those with the shortest life expectancies are generally found in pulse equipment (transponders, DME).

At any rate, it is not a bad idea—once an old navcom has been in service nine or ten years—to remove it from the panel every year or two to check its tubes. Removing the navcom from its tray usually isn't difficult; look for a pair (or two pair) of mounting screws on the unit's face. Loosen these screws just enough so you can pull the radio out (grabbing it firmly by the channel selector knobs). Then, once you've got the radio "started"—and you may find it takes a surprising amount of tugging to do this—grab it by the sides and carefully slide it all the way out of the panel. Check the back of the box to make sure the plug-in connectors are all intact.

With the radio thus removed, carefully place it in a padded box or case and take it to the local electronics-supply store, or any store that has a tube testing machine. Then, following the instructions on the machine, plug in and test your radio's tubes one by one, returning them to their proper sockets when you're done: (Don't forget to test all the tiny Nuvistor tubes scattered throughout the chassis. Some radios contain as many as two dozen of these tiny thimble-like metal tubes.) If you need help, ask the store manager. If you find a tube that's bad, you'll be faced with a dilemma: namely, you will have to choose

A surprising number of old tube-equipped, hard-wired navcoms (like this ARC unit) are still in use. If you own one, it pays to check the tubes now and then—including those many tiny Nuvistor tubes (see arrows), which cost upwards of $10 apiece and may number in the dozens.

A $1.98 spray can of color-TV contact cleaner comes in handy for cleaning contacts in older radios.

between buying a new tube and installing it yourself (which, under existing FAR's, is not exactly legal), or paying a licensed avionics technician to buy and install the new tube for you (which would be legal but expensive). Such are the choices confronting the maintenance-conscious pilot.

Before you reinstall that old navcom in your panel, take a moment to make one other maintenance check: inspect the frequency-selector wafer switches (again, this applies only to relatively ancient equipment) for cleanliness. If the contact areas are not shiny—and they probably won't be—go buy a spray can of *contact cleaner* (any electronics store can help you out), along with a package of cotton swabs, and thoroughly clean the contact points on those wafer switches. Direct a short burst of spray onto the back side of each wafer; then, using the end of a cotton swab, rub the contact areas until all of the surface oxidation has been cleaned away. When your're done, the metal contacts should shine.

After several years in service, switch contacts invariably accumulate a good deal of surface oxidation, which tends to act as an electrical barrier; obviously, it only makes sense to remove this oxidation layer periodically. (Commercial contact cleaners are designed to dissolve such oxidation while leaving behind a very thin oil layer, which acts to protect the metal from further oxidation.) If contacts are *not* periodically cleaned in this fashion, it's just a matter of time until dirt and oxidation accumulate to the point where the contacts fail to function properly. Then the next thing you know, you're taking your radio (which has mysteriously "lost" several frequencies) to the shop—and complaining about the high cost of avionics repairs. (See page 106 for more details on contact maintenance.)

With your wafer switches cleaned (and your tubes all checked out), you can now reinstall the radio in the panel. Be sure all the connectors achieve firm contact before retightening the mounting screws at the front of the set; also, be especially sure to recheck all the antenna connections. (Doublecheck to see that the master switch is *off* the whole time, too.) When you are confident that everything has been reinstalled properly, turn the switches on and verify that the set works. (If it doesn't, check the circuit-breaker panel, recheck the antenna connections, recycle all the switches, and try again. If it *still* doesn't work, you've got problems.)

Going to the Shop

Due to the nature of the failure modes that affect solid-state devices, there is only so much that any operator can do (in the way of preventive maintenance) to extend the life of avionics—and we have covered most of the applicable techniques here. Before concluding the discussion, however, we should mention some of the things you can do *after* a black box has failed (or begun to deteriorate in performance) to ensure its quick return to service.

The main thing you can do to save time, money, and aggravation on avionics repairs is communicate your needs clearly to the service technician. Before taking a radio to any repair shop, you should prepare a written brief containing answers to all of the following questions:

1. Is the set completely dead, or does it work intermittently?

2. Exactly which channels are out (if any)?

3. If the set works intermittently, does it usually fail immediately after being turned on—or several minutes later?

4. If later, *how much* later? Have you noticed a definite pattern?

5. Are you ever able to make the set regain function? How?

6. Does turning other equipment (navcoms, rotating beacons, etc.) on or off affect the behavior of the faulty set?

7. If it's a communications radio, can you transmit?

8. If it's an ADF, can you still tune and receive stations properly? Does the needle point to the station? Does the "press-to-test" button work?

9. If it's a nav unit, is your VOR error the same near the station as it is when you are farther out?

10. If the VOR head is out, are you still able to pick up the nav station signal and identify it?

11. Have you tested VOR indications in all quadrants and determined the amount of error (in degrees) for various bearings? Is the error always on the "plus" side? The "minus" side?

12. Have you tried the set on the ground with the engine on and off? Does operating the engine make any difference? Does the set behave differently on the ground than in the air?

13. Is the plane's battery in good health? (How much water has it used in the past two months?) Have you noticed any starting problems recently?

These are just some of the questions a good repair technician will want to know the answers to before examining a faulty radio. (This list of questions was, in fact, obtained from a large midwestern avionics shop; we did not make it up.)

You should, however, anticipate other questions as well, by telling the repairman whether any previous maintenance (and what kind) has been performed on the box in question, whether the alternator (or other components of the electrical system) has recently been worked on, etc.

The more things you can tell the repair technician about the defective radio's present behavior pattern, its past service history, and the circumstances under which it went kaput, the less time he will have to waste (at $25 to $50 and hour) diagnosing the problem—and the sooner you can be back in the air with a fully functional radio.

Nor should you always assume, by the way, that the radio itself is at fault. Quite often, what appears to be a bonafide radio problem actually turns out—on closer examination—to be purely an airframe or installation problem.

This is particularly true of newer-generation avionics. (If one navcom in a dual installation fails, it is common practice—and a good idea—to switch the tray location of the two sets and observe whether the problem travels with the set, or appears to be location-specific. Any problem that disappears when the radio is moved to another tray obviously involves installation.)

Many a transponder has been declared "inoperative" as a result of the antenna (which is generally mounted on the belly of the plane, not far aft of the crankcase breather line) becoming thoroughly covered with oil and dirt, thus blocking reception.

Before assuming that a particular problem resides within a particlar piece of avionics gear, check all electrical connections for security, inspect antennas (and antenna cables) for condition, check the battery for charge level, recycle all switches and circuit breakers—and even then, don't assume anything. Avionics technicians are discovering new failure modes every day.

COCKPIT SPEAKER REPLACEMENT

During a long-distance flight, an *LPM* editor suddenly discovered that his Cessna Skylane had acquired a new noise, a kind of clattering sound, the disquieting racket of something coming loose. He took off his headphones and was instantly struck by how terrifying *loud* the new noise was.

He traced the clatter to a spot just above his left ear, immediately behind the cockpit headliner: the cabin loudspeaker. In his future lay the self-imposed task of replacing the speaker. Here is how it was done—the easy parts and the hard.

Removing the Old Speaker

The left-hand cockpit loudspeaker (there's also a copilot-side speaker in the plane) had literally come unglued, where the cardboard cone sits in the metal frame. The glue around the periphery of the cone had simply dried, hardened, and deteriorated over a period of 12 years; and now, finally, the cone had separated from its frame. Normal airframe/engine vibrations were causing the free cone to clatter wildly in its metal holder.

Getting the speaker out for replacement is easy. All you have to do is loosen the plastic trim moldings at the top of the pilot's doorpost, reach a finger in behind the headliner, and (using a great deal of verbal encouragement) work the headliner material loose from its sawtooth-edged holder. If the material rips, you're still okay as long as there's enough excess headliner at the bottom so that you can tuck a bunch of it back up into the crack when you're done. (If the material rips on the *cockpit* side where you can see it, you'll have to sew in a length of patch material later on.)

After loosening the headliner, you simply fold it back to uncover the speaker, then unscrew the four speaker hold-down screws using a Phillips screwdriver, drop the speaker out, and disconnect the wires in back of it (there should be quick-disconnect junctions present). In little more than 60 seconds, you've removed the speaker from the cabin. (Quick! Put those screws back in their respective nut plates before you lose them.)

A cursory examination of the speaker showed that not only was the cone rattling around loose in its frame, but the cone itself had a three-inch rip in it. Elsewhere on the cone was a rip concealed by a layer of glue; the speaker had evidently been repaired once before at the hands of a previous owner. (Amazingly, the speaker still worked quite well, despite all the repaired and unrepaired damage.)

Got a Match?

In shopping for a replacement speaker, achieving proper hole matchup between old speaker and new was *not* difficult. The Cessna's speakers are 6 x 9-inch ovals. Their hole pattern (for mounting) matches the hole pattern of virtually all 6 x 9 speakers sold by Radio Shack, Lafayette Electronics, etc. If your speakers are 5 x 7 (or 4 x 10, etc.), chances are they will have a standard-for-that-size hold pattern.

Getting mounting holes to line up, then, is not a problem. The problem in selecting a replacement speaker is to find a speaker that matches your old one in *depth, magnet weight,* and *impedance.* Depth was a particularly severe limitation in this case (and probably in your case, if you own a Cessna), because the old speaker was just two inches thick, total, and that's all there was room for behind the headliner. A 2-5/8-inch-deep replacement speaker could not be used, for lack of room. And very few companies make a 6 x 9 speaker that's less than 2-5/8-inch deep.

Assuming you can find a replacement speaker of proper all-around size, you'll definitely want to pay attention to the mass of the magnet on the back of it, not because of weight-and-balance considerations or audio quality, but because if you replace your cockpit speaker with one that has a much bigger (or much smaller) magnet, you'll have to have your compass re-swung. Your plane's magnetic compass is quite sensitive to changes in its environment; a change in the size of your speaker magnet would certainly be "felt" by your compass.

Impedance matching is in no way critical to flight safety, but you should be aware that if you replace a 4-ohm speaker with a 16-ohm speaker, the volume controls on your radios aren't going to have the sensitivity they had before. (In fact, you may have to turn them all the way up in order to hear anything.) Try, if possible, to replace a 4-ohm speaker with a 4-ohm speaker (or something fairly close). Or buy a speaker that can be wired to give any of several impedances, including one in your desired range.

In with the New

After much running around, a 6 x 9 replacement speaker for the Skylane was located that [1] had the proper mounting hole pattern, [2] was no more than 2 inches thick, [3] weighed about the same, magnet-wise, as the old speaker, and [4] had an impedance rating of "3 to 4 ohms." The speaker is a 69C5FR aircraft replacement model made by the Quam-Nichols Company of Chicago.

After the leads from the old speaker were removed and soldered to the new one, putting the replacement loudspeaker in the airplane was anticlimactically simple (just a matter going through the removal steps in reverse). The whole process took only a couple of minutes.

It's true that you can save yourself a lot of runnng around—and a lot of frustration over impedance mismatching, magnets that are too big or too small, etc.—just by ordering a new loudspeaker through the Beech or Cessna (or Piper, etc.) dealer network. The only thing you *won't* save is money. In this case, the new speaker, which was purchased through a electronics supply firm, cost a mere 20 percent of the price demanded by Beech for a 4 x 10 replacement speaker.

TROUBLESHOOTING A STROBE SYSTEM

Strobe systems for light aircraft are simple and reliable, but like many aircraft accessories, they respond poorly to neglect. A little background knowledge will go a long way toward preventing failures, and troubleshooting them successfully when they do occur.

All conventional strobes (Whelen, Grimes, Hoskins, etc.) employ a capacitor discharge system: i.e., one or more condensers are charged to approximately 450 volts DC, then allowed to discharge across a xenon flash tube at controlled intervals. The condenser (capacitor) is parallel across the flash tube, and the flash tube is designed so that it will hold off the applied voltage until the flash is triggered by an external pulse (generally provided by a solid-state timing circuit in the power supply).

Inactivity Kills

The single most important fact you should know about getting long life from a strobe is that *strobes are meant to be used*—they deteriorate if they are left inactive (definitely a case of "use it or lose it"). A strobe power supply that has been left "off" for long periods—weeks or months—is subject to eventual failure because the electrolytic capacitors used in the device will lose polarity formation. As a rule, a strobe that has been inactive for one year can be considered elegible for sudden failure.

Electrolytic capacitors contain conducting foil layers separated by a liquid dielectric. (When a voltage is applied across the device,

Strobe lights actually deteriorate if they are not used often.

electrical energy is stored in the polarized dielectric.) Failure can occur, obviously, any time the capacitor's hermetic seal is broken, allowing dielectric to leak out. But failure also occurs when there is breakdown of the surface coating of the foil layers, which happens slowly and progressively during inactive periods. During active use, the applied voltage usually causes enough redeposition (replating) to fully restore the foil—if the surface breakdown was not excessive. After a long period of inactivity, however, the foil surface may not "reform" when a voltage is applied: instead, the voltage is dissipated as heat, and the capacitor dies.

If the airplane is not to be used for a month or more, see to it that someone at least activates the strobe power supply once every week for five to ten minutes. If this is not possible, use extreme care when first "powering up" the strobe system. Operate the power supply on a reduced voltage (75 percent of normal) for 10 to 20 minutes—this will prevent overheating of the capacitors as they reform. Should you merely turn on the strobes at full system voltage, there is an excellent chance that the capacitors will overheat and self-destruct as you taxi out for takeoff.

Basic Troubleshooting

The first step in troubleshooting any strobe system is to determine whether the trouble is in the flash tube or the power supply. This is easy, if you can substitute a known-good flash tube for the one in question. If a spare flash tube isn't available, just turn on the strobe power supply and put your ear next to it. A properly working power supply emits an audible tone (high-pitched).

Caution: Most popular strobes are protected against shorts or opens on the output, and will, in essence, shut themselves off when subjected to a flash tube that won't flash. *You* are not so protected; don't let yourself get shocked. Strobes are *high-voltage devices.* Always *let the power supply bleed down for five minutes* after shutting it off, before handling.

Also: Reversing polarity of the input power, even for an instant, will permanently damage the power supply. Such damage will not always be immediately apparent. Sometimes failure occurs later. So use care when detaching and reattaching wires to connector pins.

A good place to start if you've ruled out the flash tube as the culprit is to determine whether there is appropriate input voltage (14 or 28 volts DC, as applicable) at the power supply—something you can check with an inexpensive voltmeter.

Next, check the power supply operationally by disconnecting the output cables and connecting an operable strobe head (or bench check unit) directly to the power supply outlet. As you apply voltage to the power supply input, if the output is normal, look for problems in the interconnect cables. If red and white wires are reversed, or if a short exists between red and black wires, the power supply will be disabled until the short is cleared. (A short to ground here will not cause any lasting damage.)

Any discharge of the capacitor(s) by shorting across red (power) and white (trigger) leads *will destroy the trigger circuit.*

Harness Continuity

Continuity should be checked for each interconnect cable. (I.e., check for continuity pin one to pin one, or red connection to red connection, white to white, etc.) Also check for shorts between white and red, red and black, and black and white.

Check for shorts from any non-black wires to aircraft ground.

When the connections for red and black, or white and black, have been reversed, the system will appear to operate normally. Flash tubes will fail prematurely, however. So check for this condition, and correct it if it exists.

If the wiring checks good, the flash tube is good (see further discussion below), and appropriate voltage is getting to the power supply but the system won't operate, contact the manufacturer. All of the major manufacturers of strobe systems have in-house repair programs (not only for warranty work but out-of-warranty units). For a modest fee, you can have your power supply rebuilt to perform like new, often with a new warranty to boot. Contact SDI/Hoskins, P.O. Box 19626, Irvine, CA 92713; Grimes Div. of Midland-Ross Corp., Box 247, 550 Rt. 55, Urbana, IL 43078; or Whelen Engineering Co., Three Winter Ave., Deep River, CT 06417. Before contacting, get the model, serial number, and voltage of the unit, and be ready with a concise description of the failure mode.

Flash Tube Failure

Xenon flash tubes—aging tubes, in particular—have a number of bizarre traits that maintenance-conscious pilots should be aware of.

First, there's photosensitivity. It is not unusual for an aging xenon flash tube to be highly photosensitive—i.e., it will fire normally when exposed to bright external lighting (sunlight) but may be reluctant to fire in the dark. Also, flash tubes typically become hard-to-trigger with age. (Exposure to high temperatures can have the same effect.) You may begin to notice that a tube flashes normally with the engine running but stops firing when the engine is shut down and the system is run only on battery power. When a tube begins acting feebly in this manner, it should be replaced.

A good "quick check" of a flash tube's fitness (assuming you have a good power supply) is to operate the system on low voltage—10 volts in a 14-v airplane, or 22 volts in a 28-v system. If the tube flashes at this reduced level, it has good life remaining.

Many owners notice that when the master switch is turned off at the end of a flight, the strobes discharge spontaneously. This is normal. The flash tubes are being triggered by the voltage spike incurred with master-switch cycling. (You'd be wise, of course, to have your radios turned off at this point.)

Long-term hot/cold cycling from normal operation of the strobe system can induce eggshelling of the glass, or even leakage around the seal of the wire to the glass. Naturally, when this happens, you replace the tube.

Tubes can also go into a state of self-ionization, in which they continuously glow light-blue rather than flashing, rendering the system inoperative. Too high a charge rate in the aircraft electrical system can contribute to this syndrome.) Generally, if you turn the strobe off and then cycle it back on, it will flash a few times before quitting again (signalling reappearance of self-ionization). There's little to do at this point but buy a new tube.

Unfortunately, when you buy and install one new flash tube in any system that uses a single power supply to operate more than one tube, the presence of the new tube will often cause the remaining flash elements (if old) to misfire or skip, even though they appeared to be operating normally before. This just means that the old tubes were nearing the end of their service life. (The moral: If your system is old and fed by one power supply, you might want to consider buying replacement tubes in complete sets.)

DO-IT-YOURSELF ELT MAINTENANCE

On the whole, pilots have never been particularly happy about the legislation that has forced emergency locator transmitters upon them or with the performance of these devices. They have been even gloomier about the costs that ELTs have entailed. Still, the requirement exists and must be coped with—but there are ways of saving money in the coping.

Three Strategies

There are three basic ways of handling the equipment at least cost. The key factors are to know what is legal and how to remain within the law, to be aware of how to shop for oneself, and to be willing to take on one's own preventive maintenance.

First: Fly without an ELT if you can. A close reading of FAR 91.52 will show you that there are numerous legal ways of operating without an emergency locator transmitter. (For instance, you can choose to operate within 50 miles of home base, on "training" flights, at all times.) Our favorite escape clause is the one that says you may remove the ELT for 90 days at a time, for virtually any reason whatever—including "inspection," repair, etc.—whenever you want, so long as you put a placard in view of the pilot stating, "ELT is removed."

Second: Don't let your mechanic or FBO go battery-shopping for you at annual-inspection time. Do the shopping yourself and save money. Two prime sources are G.R. Lowe, of Clinton, Missouri, and Merl, Inc., Box 188, Meriden, Connecticut 06450.

Third: *Replace out-of-date ELT power packs yourself.* (It's entirely legal as preventive maintenance.) This operation is so unbelievably simple that it's hard to imagine that anyone would actually pay a mechanic to do it.

Disassembly

The Narco ELT-10 is fairly typical of emergency beacons in general with regard to its battery-change procedure. (If you own a Sharc 7 or Merl unit, the following steps will be mostly the same for you.) Always start by disarming the transmitter—the switch, find the switch!—and removing it from the airplane. If an external antenna is connected, disconnect it by twisting the coax cable gently, then pulling it straight out. Unstrap the ELT from its tray, and it should come free.

If a portable (tape-type) antenna is present, deploy it as far as it will extend.

You can get a good idea of how your transmitter assembles and disassembles from its power pack simply by studying the replacement power pack at this point. You may be somewhat surprised (downright amazed?) to find that the replacement "battery" is almost as big, by itself, as the entire assembled unit. The Narco ELT-10 battery pack, for example, weighs in at 2.8 pounds—while the transmitter-and-battery combo, by comparison, totals 3.3 pounds. That 5-ounce end-piece with the OFF/ON/ARM switch and the RESET button is the electronic "guts" of the ELT. *That's* your emergency transmitter.

At this point, you need to detach the transmitter from the old (out of date) or worn-out (used for more than one hour, total) battery pack. This can be accomplished with the aid of a small screwdriver, a Swiss army knife, or (breakaway torque permitting) a very stout fingernail. Remove the hold-down screws and set them where they absolutely, positively won't get lost.

Next, pull gently on the transmitter to separate it from the power pack. As you pull, you'll notice two wires (red and black) emanating from within the old pack, running up to a pair of snaps on the transmitter's circuit board. The snaps are familiar to you, if you've ever owned a cheap transistor radio. Congratulations: now you own a very expensive transistor radio.

Pry the snaps apart with your fingers. Then give the old battery pack a decent burial (do not cremate—incineration can be dangerous).

Reassembly

The new power pack snaps into place right where the old one came out, naturally. After snapping the new one in, look to see if your new

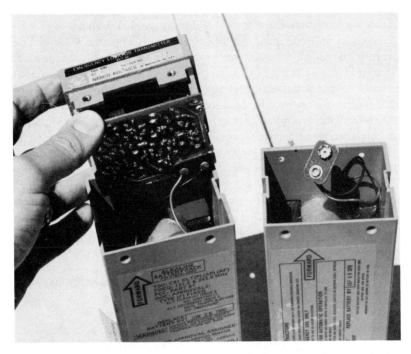

The transmitter portion of the ELT is the small, five-ounce piece attached to one end (or side) of the power pack. Here, a Narco ELT-10 is shown at left, with its replacement battery pack waiting at right.

battery came with a little plastic baggy filled with something resembling Vaseline. If so, smear some of this stuff around the edges of your transmitter's case; then slide the transmitter onto the end of the power pack, wipe off any excess Vaseline, and reinstall those tiny hold-down screws. (The jelly sealant gives your ELT a water-tight, gas-tight seal for maximum protection against corrosion.)

Now reinstall the entire unit in the airplane, going through all the removal steps in reverse order. Press the RESET button, if any; then, *at the top of the hour* (when it is legal, for five minutes, to set your ELT off accidentally), return the activation switch from OFF to ARM. Verify that your ELT isn't actually transmitting in the ARM mode by turning your master switch and number one radio on (select 121.5 MHz) briefly.

Before you make your logbook entry, you should do one more thing: You should verify that the just-worked-on ELT is in good working order (*will* transmit) by briefly turning the activation switch to ON while someone across the field monitors 121.5 MHZ—again, at zero to five minutes past the top of the hour. This check should be performed using a receiving radio some distance away from the ELT. (If your ELT is working but your external ELT antenna isn't, your own plane's navcoms will still pick up a normal-sounding signal during the test due to close proximity alone. That's not what you want to hear. You want someone *miles away* to be able to pick up your ELT signal in an emergency, and that's possible only if the external antenna is functional.) Incidentally, if you don't *have* an external (airframe) antenna for your ELT, get one. Most manufacturers now require it.

Now make your logbook entry and paste the "battery reminder" sticker in the front of your airframe log. And congratulate yourself on saving $10 to $50 on ELT maintenance. (And: Hope like heck you never need the dumb device.)

MAINTAINING CONTACTS

Everyone needs good contacts. Remember the sequence in propping a plane? Brakes set, mags on, and, like an ace in a World War I fighter flick, you say the potent word, "Contact!"

Why do you say that?

Because the action of turning on the magnetos involves the touching together of two small pieces of metal inside the mag switch. The switch *contacts*.

Your modern airplane is replete with contacts. they are the points of activation between your will and your radios, landing gear, and anything else electrical you switch on and off. They are sensitive and vulnerable. They need protection.

As anyone who's dealt with crud-caked battery terminals knows, bad electrical connections take their toll in performance. Your battery may be fully charged, but if the connections to it are corroded, you'll have trouble cranking your engine. And so it is with other electrical connections.

Solid connections, left untouched, might not give trouble for years. But switches—pairs of electrical *contacts* that open and close—offer unique opportunities for mayhem. By their very nature, they are "open" and exposed to (atmospheric) oxygen, moisture, and impurities (dirt, pollen, lint) much of the time; they are subject to electrical arcing; heating and cooling take place in normal use; and friction forces occur during each switch cycling. All of which sets the stage for contamination, corrosion, and physical damage.

Sealed microswitch, commonly found in gear systems, hides its contacts.

Happily, most switch contacts are in protected areas (many switches, such as landing gear microswitches, battery relays—or "contactors"—and starter relays, are in fact sealed units), and these problems are minimized. But others are not so protected; they benefit from occasional cleaning.

What Is a Contact?

Let's begin with the basics. A contact is two pieces of metal so arranged as to allow an external force to cause the metal pieces to touch ("closed") or not touch ("open").

Ideally, there should be zero opposition (or resistance) to current flow across the contacts when they are closed, infinite resistance when they are open, and they should *break* (open) and *make* (closed) freely.

The most common example of a contact is the old familiar toggle switch used for everything from mags to map lights. Variations of this switch lead us to push-buttons, rockers, rotary key-operated, and push-pull. They all operate on the same principle: When you push them (or pull them, or rock them or rotate them, they will cause two pieces of metal either to touch or not touch. Slightly more exotic are the PTT switch contacts inside a microphone case, the gear "squat" and uplock swiches, the radio on/off switch, and the radio channel selector switch.

There is another category of switch that you may not think of as a switch, but it is, really, just another way of causing two pieces of metal to make contact. This switch, though, is not directly hand-operated, but depends on the principle of electromagnetism to pull the two metal contacts together. This is the good old relay, or electromagnetic switch. The most common examples are the voltage regulator and the transmit-receive relay in the transceiver. You may not immediately think of the master battery relay, the starter solenoid, or the multitude of solenoids and relays in the autopilot.

Contacts need protection because when they corrode sufficiently, they open the circuit, no matter how energetically the pilot tries to close it. Actually, there are two forces at work—dirt and actual corrosion—but they can be treated simply as corrosion. As we have seen in our earlier discussion of corrosion, a little cleaning goes a long way in thwarting this menace, if the proper methods and substances are used.

Alcohol Cleaning

Landing gear switches are usually of the sealed "micro" variety. Even with the protection afforded by a sealed case, however, the aircraft wheels nonetheless throw enough mud and grime into the wells that sooner or later *some* dirt inevitably finds its way into the switch housing.

For the most part, the only "cure" for this is prevention or replacement. Still, when you wash your airplane, do your gear switches a favor and hose the crud from around them.

What if you suspect a fouled switch? According to Jim Weir, of Radio Systems Technology, there may be hope: "One last-ditch effort that proves successful in about half the cases is to soak the switch in rubbing alcohol, or even vodka, for a day, dry it with compressed air, and test it with an ohmmeter. If it 'makes' with one ohm or less, and 'breaks'—with a megohm or more—as you press the button, the switch is as good as new and you can reinstall it to the gear."

Weir advises that if the switch fails the alcohol test, throw it back into the alcohol for a few hours. "After a few hours, with the switch still submerged, press the activation button a few dozen times, remove it, dry it, and try the ohmmeter test a few times."

(Weir cautions that the alcohol bath should not be tried on any switch containing polystyrene parts, since alcohol can dissolve polystyrene.)

Corrosion Chemistry

The alcohol bath technique works fine for dirt. True corrosion is more than surface-deep, however, and requires appropriate countermeasures—in some cases, chemical warfare.

Corrosion, of course, is nothing more than the (inevitable) process of a metal trying to combine itself with the oxygen, moisture, and other constituents of the atmosphere. In urban areas, sulfur dioxide occurs in relatively high amounts, as well as sulfuric acid. Both of these substances are among the most active corrosion-producers known. The rate of attack depends on the contact material.

The precious metals (gold, silver, platinum, palladium, rhodium) are about as impervious to corrosion as any metals anywhere—all take months or years to form an oxide coating—and for this reason, most switch contacts are made from precious metals, or at the very least, *plated* with them. The least chemically reactive metal—gold—never forms an oxide or sulfide layer, and so gold is the best contact material available. It's also the most expensive. If you've ever wondered why certain switches and relays cost so much, this is one reason. (Legend has it that King's Gold Crown series radios are so named—and so priced—because more far more gold is used in them, on connectors and switch contacts, than in the cheaper Silver Crown line.)

Why not use common metals, like aluminum or copper? Because all common metals—iron, aluminum, copper, tin, zinc, cadmium, etc.—spontaneously form a surface layer of oxide (or sulfide) within hours of exposure to air (or smog). And the metal oxides, it turns out, are all relatively good insulators. Thus, a corroded base-metal switch would never be able to close its contacts and "make" a good electrical connection—a thin layer of oxide (something like a thin layer of air) is formed between the metal contacts, effectively creating a permanent "open" switch.

Ordinarily, a quality switch will have a silver, silver-palladium, or silver-cadmium surface, with possibly a micron-thick layer of gold plating over the surface. (Magneto breaker points used to be fabricated from platinum and iridium, in the radial engine's heyday; now, for economy reasons, tungsten alloy is used.) The trick to cleaning a set of contacts, therefore, becomes one of removing the dirt and oxide layer *without removing any of the precious-metal surface.* Obviously, with gold-plated contacts, the potential exists for a hamhanded technician to strip the gold from the contacts on the very first cleaning attempt. Then the underlying silver alloy will tarnish rapidly, and before you know it, you wind up having to clean the contacts quite often. (If—heaven forbid—you break through the silver layer to the base metal below, your contact life may be shortened to a few days or hours.)

Approved Cleaners

The FAA is strangely silent on the subject of contact cleaning. But according to Weir, "The very best cleaner for any small contact, such as in transceiver relays, microphone switches, and the like, is *bond* typewriter paper and alcohol or a good grade of color-TV tuner cleaner." Bond paper, says Weir, has just enough surface irregularities to be a very mild abrasive. "The idea," he explains, "is to soak a strip of the paper with the alcohol or color-TV tuner cleaner, then place the wet paper between the contacts, close the contacts manually, and slowly draw the paper through the contacts. The contacts, when you

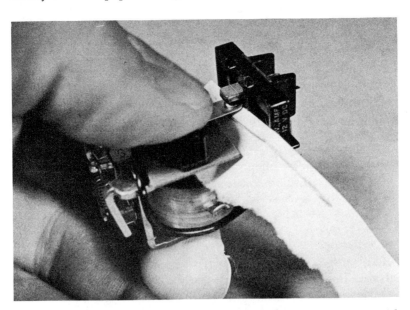

Relay contacts can be cleaned by wetting a piece of bond typing paper with alcohol and pulling the paper through the closed contacts. That dark stripe on the paper is corrosion.

do this, should have just enough closing pressure to permit the paper to be pulled with a slight drag."

The bond-paper and tuner-cleaner trick, incidentally, is approved by magneto manufacturers as a way of removing tungsten oxide corrosion from magneto breaker points. (Dressing with a stone is *not* approved.)

For larger, non-plated contacts such as in voltage regulators, the answer is something called a "burnishing tool," which sells for a buck or two at most any TV or electornics *supply* shop (i.e., Radio Shack or the equivalent). The tool is simply a mild abrasive strip with a plastic handle. Used with a little alcohol (and a little discretion), it will do the trick for most medium- and heavy-duty contact-dressing jobs. Burnishing tools come in various qualities and styles; the ones we're talking about are inexpensive. If you want to, you can splurge on one of the diamond-dust-blade models often sold in electronics stores at Neiman-Marcus prices (bring your Gold Card), but it's not necessary.

Arcing and Friction

Arcing and friction play a role in keeping contact surfaces clean (which means that exercising switches regularly, with the master switch on, is a good preventive measure). If a fair amount of current is switched by the contacts—a quarter-amp or more—the contacts will be self-cleaning and shouldn't require manual cleaning very often, if at all. The reason: a very tiny arc occurs for a few milliseconds during the time the switch is opened, and this arc is enough to melt and vaporize any small amount of dirt and/or corrosion that may have accumulated at the surface of the contact. In addition, a very small amount of the contact surface actually melts and reflows, so that the switch makes a new contact surface every time it is opened. (There can be too much of a good thing, however. When a low-rated switch is used in a high-flow circuit—as when a Cessna 152's battery contactor is accidentally swapped with the starter contactor—the contact "melt" can be excessive, and the surface metal can vaporize and disappear. The actual measured life of a 1-amp switch in a 20-amp circuit was, in one instance, two toggles.)

Friction is also a factor in the self-cleaning action of many switches. Push-button, push-pull, and rotary types all have a mode of action in which the contacts wipe themselves clean by a physical rubbing together of the contact surfaces. Where problems occur is when a "dry" (or current-less) circuit is switched with a toggle-type switch.

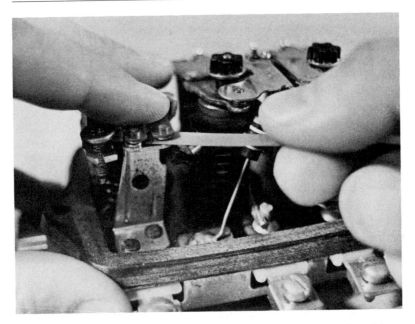

Contact-dressing tool (similar to a nail file, only finer) can be purchased from any electronics store for $1.98 to tens of dollars (for diamond-dust models). Here, a voltage regulator's points are being dressed. Always wet the tool's blade with alcohol or contact cleaner.

Toggle switches, unlike the others mentioned above, do not wipe themselves clean and thus continue to gather corrosion continuously. In a dry circuit, with no significant current to supply an arc, the contacts eventually develop a high resistance and fail to close (and "make") the circuit. And since toggles are usually sealed, it's impossible to clean the contacts manually. There is, nevertheless, a preventive-maintenance technique to deal with toggle switches. Weir describes a commonly used shop trick: "What you do is remove the circuit wires from the switch and hook the switch up in parallel with the nav-light switch, using alligator clips. It doesn't have to be the nav-light circuit—any medium-current-load circuit will do. Using the bad switch, turn the lights on and off a half-dozen times. This should 'arc' the contacts clean."

If the foregoing trick doesn't restore the switch's function, Weir says, it's probably because the oxide layer is too thick to be induced to arc off by a 12-volt electrical system. (Owners of 24-volt aircraft should have good success with the method.) "If you still want to save the switch," advises Weir, "you will have to use a high voltage at a few milliamperes."

Wafer Switches

In transceivers (and many other radios), there are wafer switches to contend with. You can tell when a channel-selector wafer is getting dirty when you have to rotate to the same channel a half-dozen times to get it to work (or when you have to hold the selector knob slightly off-center to make it work). Once again, color-TV tuner cleaner is the solvent of choice. It comes in a spray can, cleans rapidly, and evaporates without a trace. (Also, the solvents in it will not attack plastics used in radios—although if you spray any on a *hot* tube, you may crack it.) Wafers have a self-wiping action, so the thing to do is spray a small, directed quantity of tuner cleaner at the contact area, then rapidly rotate the selector switch. Cotton swabs (also available at your electronics supply store) can be used to "mop up" the dissolved corrosion.

A word to the wise: Most commercially available color-TV tuner sprays have a slight perfume odor. If you have a switch problem that aerosol tuner cleaner *doesn't* fix, and you end up having to take your radio to an avionics shop, first let it sit out in the fresh air for a day or so to allow the perfume to evaporate. "Most shops are death on do-it-yourselfers," Jim Weir notes, "and they may well refuse to work on a 'perfumed' radio."

Careful maintenance can clean up electronic areas that chronically cause inconvenience. As the next chapter will show, alternators and generators are similarly susceptible to reform.

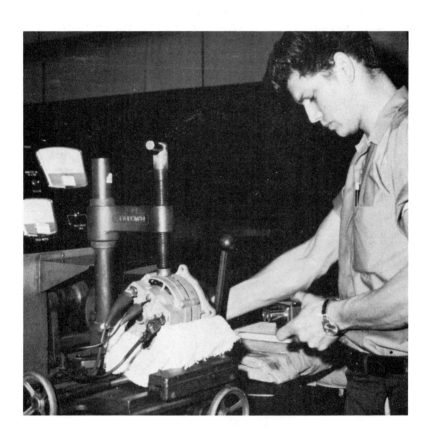

Chapter 5

ALTERNATORS AND GENERATORS

Losing your alternator or generator can be a problem ranging from the inconvenient to the catastrophic. If you are flying immersed in cloud, the threat of losing your communications and electronic navigation capability can be a nightmarish lump in the pit of the stomach as you try to figure how much longer your battery has to live, which devices to turn off and which to leave on, and what further options are left to you.

Alternator and generator failures are frequent enough for many pilots to accept them stoically. Some pilots view them less philosophically—unless their rage can be considered existential. Not only does flying with the fact of alternator vulnerability generate broadly different responses to the problem. So does pondering the alternatives that come with servicing.

ALTERNATORS

It has been said that there are two schools of thought on alternator servicing. One school says that if the problem is confined to the alternator, it should be exchanged out or replaced. The other school, by contrast, says that since most alternator glitches are of a minor nature and can easily be repaired once they are diagnosed, the thing to do is repair the defective unit. The latter approach is often more cost-effective. The trick is knowing when it's *not* the wisest route to go.

Unfortunately, alternators get blamed for a lot of electrical problems that have nothing to do with the alternator itself. Voltage regulators, static wicks, improperly tensioned drive belts, corroded battery posts, and overly sensitive over-voltage sensors (a particular problem in late-model Cessna singles) are all quite often culprits in false-alarm "bad alternator" episodes. In many cases, a quick bench check would have exonerated the alternator right off the bat (or right off the "BAT").

The best, surest way to implicate—or exonerate—an alternator in any electrical-system problem is, of course, to replace the suspect alternator (temporarily) with a known-good one, to see if the problem disappears with removal of the old alternator. This may not always be convenient, unfortunately.

The Trouble Is . . .

Generally speaking, alternator troubles fall into a relatively few categories. We will intentionally neglect bearing trouble here, since this is strictly a mechanical difficulty and its remedy is obvious. Of the typical alternator problems per se, diode failure is fairly common. (As you know, diodes are used to convert an alternator's AC output into DC power for use in the airplane's electrical system.) The main symptom, in this case, is considerably reduced electrical output as seen on the aircraft ammeter, or low charging voltage under heavy electrical load, possibly combined with a whining noise over the cockpit speaker. To confirm the diagnosis, place an ohmmeter across the "B" terminal of the alternator and the alternator case (all systems off). Reverse the probes. There should be an infinite resistance in at least one direction. (Note: Failed alternator diodes are most often shorted, rather than open.)

If the above test shows an infinite resistance in *both* directions, repeat the test using a hot-light type continuity tester. Some ohmmeters produce insufficient voltage at the probes to forward-bias a diode, in which case you'll get a very high resistance in either direction using an ohmmeter—but continuity in only *one* direction with a hot-light.

Another fairly common problem with aircraft alternators is an open field circuit, caused either by severely worn brushes or by an actual open in the rotor field winding. Here again, detection is easy. Connecting an ohmmeter across the "F" terminal and alternator case, and rotating the alternator shaft, you should see 12 to 20 ohms of resistance. More, and you've got trouble.

Sometimes a break in the field winding occurs at the point where the field winding connects to the slip ring—in which case resoldering the connection will usually cure the problem. In other cases, deposits may build up in the brush holder and prevent the brush (or brushes) from touching the slip rings. Either way, the primary symptom will, of course, be a total lack of alternator output.

By contrast, a *shorted* field winding usually shows up as a popped field or alternator regulator circuit breaker. (The diagnosis is con-

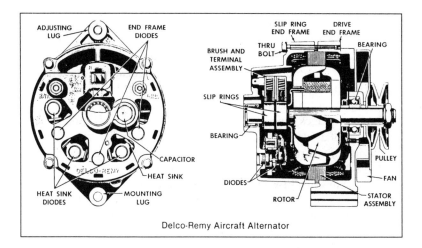

Delco-Remy Aircraft Alternator

firmed if an ohmmeter check of "F" terminal to case shows less than five ohms.)

Shorted stator windings occasionally occur, the main symptom being reduced output (low ammeter). This type of problem is most often found by process of elimination: If all diodes check good and, on teardown, there is evidence of overheating in one or more stator windings, it is usually safe to assume that a short has occurred in a winding. Some caution should be exercised here, however; a discolored winding is not always evidence of overheating (sometimes it's just old age). Use the time-honored *fingernail test*: If the winding's insulation can be flaked off with a fingernail, the winding has been overheated.

You often hear of an alternator with an open "Y". The symptom is total lack of alternator output. Such a condition is best confirmed visually, with the alternator taken apart. The "Y" connection point will be charred or discolored due to overheating, and in many cases, the connection will be obviously loose. Often, cleaning and recrimping (or soldering) the "Y" connection results in a satisfactory repair.

Testing

A hot-light (a simple continuity tester consisting of a bulb, two probes, and a battery) works well for checking field-coil continuity in the rotor and performing other bench checks. To check field-coil continuity, simply touch the hot-light's test leads across the alternator's field coil terminals. (Note: One side is often connected to ground.) If the light fails to come on, then obviously there is poor continuity and you have located a problem. The lack of continuity could be due to poor brush contact on the slip rings, or an open field winding. To pinpoint the problem, remove the brush holder or rotor assembly and touch your test leads directly to the slip rings. If there's still no light, you've got an open field winding in the rotor.

The above check can, of course, also be done with an ohmmeter. The advantage of using an ohmmeter is that you can obtain a fairly precise resistance measurement in place of the all-or-nothing information registered by a hot-light. Typical field coil resistance is in the range of five to ten ohms for 12-volt alternators, and somewhat higher for some 24-volt alternators. Obviously, an on-the-aircraft check of coil resistance—with meter leads connected across the "F" terminal and alternator case—is actually being made through the alternator's field brushes, so that the accuracy of the reading is highly dependent on the condition of the brushes, the brushes' contact area, etc. (This is why the aircraft manufacturers tell you to make you on-the-aircraft ohmmeter check with the *rotor turning*.) A better procedure is to dismount the alternator and make your measurement directly on the slip rings. Unfortunately, this is not always convenient.

A few words of caution when making on-the-aircraft checks of an alternator:

1. Do not attempt to polarize an aircraft alternator.

2. Do not short across or ground any terminals in the charging circuit.

3. Never operate the system with the output terminal open-circuited and the field circuit energized.

4. Observe proper ground polarity with alternator, regulator, and battery. (U.S. aircraft are negative-grounded, just like domestic automobiles.)

Also, it helps to have clean connections everywhere. And your alternator belt (if belt-driven) should be snug. (Always recheck a new belt after the first ten or 20 hours in service; they do loosen up.) Pulleys, likewise, should be in track and parallel. Check this by laying a straightedge across each, touching both pulleys at once. They should be perfectly true.

Peak-to-Peak Voltage Testing

Every technician knows (or should know) that the best way to check an alternator is with an oscilloscope. There's a very good reason for

Delco-Remy Alternator Troubleshooting			
COMPONENT	CONNECTION	READING	RESULTS
Rotor	Ohmmeter from slip ring to shaft	Very low	Grounded
	110 volt test lamp from slip ring to shaft	Lamp lights	Grounded
	Ohmmeter across slip rings	Very high	Open
	110 volt test lamp across slip ring	Lamp fails to light	Open
	Battery and ammeter to slip rings, across slip rings	Compare voltmeter and ammeter readings	Compare with specifications in 1G-186 for shorts
Stator	Ohmmeter from lead to frame	Very low	Grounded
(Disconnected from diodes)	110 volt test lamp from lead to frame	Lamp lights	Grounded
	Ohmmeter across each pair of leads	Any reading very high	Open
	110 volt test light across each pair of leads	Fails to light	Open
Diode	Ohmmeter across diode, then reverse connections	Both readings very low	Shorted
(Disconnected from diodes)		Both readings very high	Open
	14 or 28-volt test lamp across diode, then reverse connections	Lamp fails to light in both checks	Open
		Lamp lights in both checks	Shorted

this: The output of an alternator is not pure direct current (DC). Instead, it is actually pulsating DC, also described as DC with a *ripple* voltage. This ripple is visible on an oscilloscope, which vaguely resembles a small television set with a serious outgrowth of knobs and switches, and which might justifiably be called an engineer's "Magic Slate."

It also happens that there's a specialized kind of alternating-current (AC) voltmeter called a *peak-to-peak* voltmeter. If connected to the output of an alternator, such a unit is capable of indicating the maximum value of the ripple voltage (i.e., the difference between the peaks) independently of the DC component. While a standard AC voltmeter would also conceivably work in this case, its reading would not be as sharply defined as the peak-to-peak meter's reading, since

Rewinding an alternator's stator windings is a skill the owner would like to avoid paying for, if he can avoid frying the windings in the first place by attention to the alternator's initial trouble signs.

the conventional AC voltmeter or ammeter actually indicates the so-called root-mean-square (RMS) value of the signal, which is .707 times the peak value in the case of a pure sinusoidal waveform.

The reason these considerations are important in alternator testing is that an alternator with a faulty diode (one of the most common sources of trouble) produces a very sharp spike, or spike pattern, of voltage and current. These spikes are not of sufficient duration to have much effect on the RMS-indicating (conventional AC) voltmeter. A peak-to-peak meter, on the other hand, will show a strong reaction to these spikes.

There is a portable, fairly inexpensive peak-to-peak voltmeter on the market designed to test alternator diodes in the dynamic condition. The new unit, called to Support Systems Analyzer, clamps onto your plane's alternator (with the alternator in the airplane) and gives a meter readout of peak-to-peak voltage output as you run your engine at 1,000 to 1,500 rpm. In a matter of minutes, you can test your alternator for function under load, without the aid of a scope, and determine whether diode failure (undetectable with your plane's ammeter) has occurred. (In this sense, the Support Systems Analyzer is a kind of poor man's oscilloscope.)

The advantage of this kind of instrument, aside from its low cost, is its ability to indicate a faulty diode even when conventional load tests or voltage tests fail to do so. A single blown diode can easily reduce an alternator's output by ten percent, which might not be considered significant. (A voltmeter test of the system would also likely be within limits.) Yet, with one diode gone bad, the other diodes—laboring under increased load—are almost certain to follow, *if* the alternator's windings don't fry in the meantime.

Why not simply check the diodes with a conventional ohmmeter

Alternator Output Specs (Delco-Remy)			
Alternator	1100660	1100717	1100718
Delco-Remy Ref. Serv. Bulletin	1G-186, 1G-262	1G-187, 1G-262	1G-187, 1G-262
Field Current (80°F)			
Amps	2.2 - 2.6	2.2 - 2.6	1.2 - 1.3
Volts	12.0	12.0	24.0
Cold Output:			
Spec. Volts	14.0	14.0	24.0
Amps	25	25	6
Approx. RPM	2000	2000	2000
Amps	65	65	46
Approx. RPM	5000	5000	5000

and be done with it? First of all, it is not always possible to gain access to the diodes without opening up the alternator on a bench. Second, there is no guarantee that a diode that checks good on the ohmmeter will not break down under load. The silicon diodes commonly used in alternators have a forward conduction turn-on voltage of 0.7 volt. Most ohmmeters operate from a 1.5-volt battery; 4.5- to 9-volt sources are used on the highest resistance range. These very low voltages are indeed enough to discriminate between the forward and the reverse modes, but they are not sufficient to break down the junction in the reverse mode, if it is weak.

It is important to recall that the output from an alternator can easily exceed 100 volts if it is not held in constant check by a voltage/current regulator and the rectifying diodes. A diode which passes the low-voltage ohmmeter test could very well fail when subjected to the high forward and back voltages experienced in normal operation.

It should be noted that the Support Systems Analyzer, in addition to measuring peak-to-peak voltages, has two selectable DC ranges (for checking regulator function). Thus, the device—while designed primarily as a rectifier dynamic tester—also functions as a DC voltmeter.

We agree with the manufacturer's basic premise, which is that most

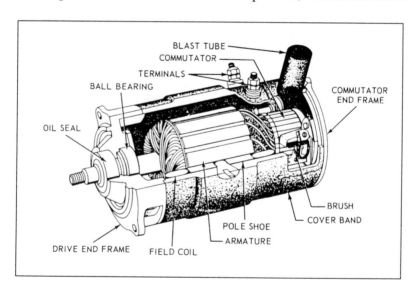

The generator is simpler than the alternator, but output equates to rpm.

A&Ps aren't equipped with proper tools for testing alternators (oscilloscopes, etc.), and that many alternator diode failures go unnoticed until it's too late. Who knows how many stator windings (and/or navcoms, DMEs, etc.) might be saved through regular use of a peak-to-peak voltage checker?

Where to Get Repairs

Many engine shops and FBOs perform minor alternator repairs, such as replacement of diodes. If yours does not, you have several options. You can remove your alternator, send it out to a local automotive accessory repair shop, and have the repaired unit checked and reinstalled by an A&P (you'd be surprised how many A&Ps send their customers' alternators and generators to local auto shops for repair); you can attempt a repair yourself, under the guidance of an appropriately skilled A&P; or you can send the defective unit off for overhaul or exchange to one of the country's many large accessory shops.

KEEPING YOUR DC GENERATOR ALIVE

If your aircraft is equipped with a DC generator (a many are), you're in for some good news ... and some bad news. The good news is that generators are, as electrical accessories go, fairly reliable. The bad news is that they are nowhere near as reliable as alternators (100-amp Crittendens notwithstanding), and to get long life out of your generator you're going to have to service it regularly.

Unfortunately, most aircraft service manuals do not have a great deal to say on the subject of periodic generator inspection and/or servicing. Your shop manual will tell you how to remove and install the generator; and, no doubt, you'll come across the recommendation that your generator (or alternator) be replaced at each engine major-overhaul period. Which is fine. But what do you do to keep your generator in top shape during those 1,500 to 2,000 hours *between* engine overhauls?

We'd like to make the following suggestions, based on our own knowledge of generators and on information compiled by Piper Aircraft Corporation.

First, establish a regular inspection interval for your generator, based on your own knowledge of the service demands being placed on the unit. (If your generator sees heavy use, plan on inspecting it every 100 hours.) Remember that high-speed operation, high ambient temperatures, operation in dusty environments, and frequent operation of the generator at or near full output are all factors which increase bearing, commutator, and brush wear.

Second, stick with your inspection schedule once you've decided on one. The inspection itself needn't take long. Obviously, you'll want to check the generator belt for proper tension (and satisfactory physical appearance); as a rule of thumb, you should see 5/16 of an inch (or 8mm) of deflection when a 10-pound load is applied at right angles to the belt midway between pulleys.

How to Check Belt Tension

Generator and alternator drive belts, when properly installed and tensioned, can be relied upon to give hundreds of hours of trouble-free operation. But, as pointed out in a Lycoming service publication (S.I. 1129A, dated February 27, 1970), "an improperly tensioned belt will wear rapidly and may slip and reduce electrical energy output." Because generator belts tend naturally to loosen somewhat with time, Lycoming and Continental both recommend that belt tension be checked not only at the time of initial installation, but after 25 hours of operation and every 100 hours thereafter.

One way to check belt tension is with a belt tension gauge made for that purpose; this is not practical, however, for most pilot/owners. A much more practical way to check belt tension is with a torque wrench. Simply fit a torque wrench and socket to the nut that attaches the generator pulley to the generator (or alternator), and begin turning the nut in a clockwise direction. The idea is to measure the *amount of torque required to make the pulley slip against the belt.* This torque should correspond to the values given in the accompanying table. If the observed torque is lower than the values listed in the table, the belt is loose and should be tightened. Conversely, if you find that it takes a *lot* of torque to slip the belt, it's too tight. (Notice that the minimal slippage torque ranges somewhat lower for old belts than new belts.)

Note: Avco Lycoming advises that "although the specified torque values for DC generators and alternators are the

Checking Generator Belt Tension		
Belt width	Con- dition	Slippage torque at generator pulley
3/8 in.	New	11 to 13 ft. lbs.
1/2 in.	New	13 to 15 ft. lbs.
3/8 in.	Old	7 to 9 ft. lbs.
1/2 in.	Old	9 to 11 ft. lbs.

same, the tension for alternator belts should be slightly higher than the tension applied to DC generator belts." (See Lycoming S.I. 1129A.)

There's only one problem with the torque method of ascertaining belt tension (aside from the fact that in some installations, easy wrench access to the generator pulley is unavailable): You can't use this method with Chrysler alternators. As luck (or perversity) would have it, Chrysler alternators do not have a nut on the drive shaft. You can't fit a torque wrench onto the shaft or the pulley.

The alternative to the torque/slip method is, of course, the tried-and-true *deflection method*. Here, you simply hook a fishing scale to the drive belt (midway between pulleys) and pull on the scale until a reading of 10 pounds is obtained (or 14 pounds, if the belt is less than 25 hours old). Using a ruler, measure the belt's deflection under a 10-pound load. It should be no less than 5/16 of an inch, and no more than 3/8 of an inch.

If you should encounter a belt that appears to be under-tensioned or over-tensioned, examine it closely for cracks and/or signs of delamination. Old belts may be retightened or replaced (as necessary) using the same basic methods you would use to tighten or replace a fan belt on your car, except that [1] you'll want to keep the hammering and banging to a minimum, and [2] you will want an A&P mechanic to sign off the work when you're done. (There is some question as to whether the FAA sees belt replacement as a type of preventive maintenance.)

A couple of words of caution are in order regarding belt replacement. First, be sure to loosen the generator (or alternator) enough so you won't have to drag the new belt over the pulley sheaves. Forcing belts over sheaves reduces belt life dramatically. Don't do it. Secondly, be sure—if there's an arrow printed on the belt—that the belt is installed so the arrow points in the direction of belt travel.

Particular Items to Check

In addition to belt tension, you'll also want to pay particular attention to the following inspection items:

1. Check all external connections and wiring; replace deteriorated grommets. Ensure that nearby wires, hoses, etc. cannot short across generator terminals. Secure loose wires with tie-wraps or clamps as appropriate.

2. Check the security of the generator's mounting by grabbing it and shaking it. There should be no "give." Inspect mounting brackets for cracks. Lycoming advises that "service experience has shown that

looseness [of generator mounting brackets] could result in a cracked crankcase."

3. Remove the cover band from the generator so that the commutator, brushes, and internal connections are inspectable. If the commutator is dirty, you can clean it with a small strip of No. 00 sandpaper (*not* emery cloth). Simply press the sandpaper against the commutator with a stick (wood, not metal) while the generator is rotating, working the sandpaper back and forth across the face of the commutator. (It is not recommended that you do this while the engine is running. Remove the generator from the aircraft or find a way to turn the generator over without operating the engine.) After sanding, throughly blow out the generator with compressed air.

Note: If the commutator is rough or out of round or obviously burned, pitted, etc., it is highly advisable to remove and disassemble the generator so that the commutator can be turned down in a lathe.

If your commutator looks healthy, wipe it down with a Varsol-moistened cloth (unleaded gasoline is okay too) to remove surface grime and oxidation. A periodic wipe-down will keep grime from accumulating to the point where generator output slowly (and insidiously) begins to taper off.

4. The final item in your periodic generator inspection should be to check the *brushes* and *brush tension*. If visual access to the brushes is poor, stick your finger(s) into the generator and *feel* their length. The best way to gauge brush wear is simply to buy your next set of brushes now (not later), and compare your existing brushes to the new ones. Most of the Delco generators in use on light aircraft today require new brushes when the old ones have worn to a length of *one-half inch* (13 millimeters) or less.

The important thing to remember when installing new brushes is that the new brush must be seated properly (that is, it must be seated to at least 75 percent of the contact surface) before the generator is returned to service. One way of doing this is to start the engine, immediately turn the master switch OFF, and let the engine idle for 15 minutes or so. After 15 or 20 minutes of operation, the new brushes will have seated sufficiently that you can turn the master switch on and begin utilizing the generator again.

Another, quicker way of seating new brushes is to break them in with sandpaper. Most service manuals advise against the use of any kind of abrasive to seat new brushes, but it is common practice, nonetheless, to place a strip of No. 0000 sandpaper between the

Generator Output Specifications (Delco-Remy)

Generator model	1101915	1101905	1105055
Delco-Remy Ref. Serv. Bulletin	1G-150	1G-150	1G-150
Brush Spring Tension	24 oz.	24 oz.	28 oz.
Field Current (80°F)			
Amps	1.62-1.72	0.75-0.85	1.45-1.55
Volts	12	24	24
Cold Output			
Amps	50	25	50
Volts	14.0	26.0	28.5
Approx. RPM	3960	3550	3730

commutator and brush (rough side facing the brush) and seat the brush by pulling the sandpaper in the direction of commutator rotation by hand. (The idea is to pull the sandpaper through several times, keeping it in the exact contour of the commutator, so that the new brushes end up having exactly the right shape.) If you go this route, be sure that you blow out the generator with compressed air afterwards.

Brush tension should be checked whether your brushes are old or new; excessive spring tension will lead to rapid brush (and commutator) wear, while low tension will cause arcing and pitting of the commutator.

If you catch low brush tension in time, you can save yourself the expense (and downtime) of having the commutator turned down later. How do you know what the proper tension is—and how do you measure it? The correct spring tension for your generator's brushes is given (along with other service test specifications) in the appropriate Delco-Remy service bulletin (consult your mechanic or write Delco-Remy, 2401 Columbus Ave., Anderson, IN 46011).

Most Delco units have recommended brush tension in the 24 to 28-ounce range as measured with a spring scale hooked on the brush arm or brush attaching screw.

Be sure the brush spring bears centrally on the top of the brushes, ensuring full brush contact with the commutator.

Also, before attempting to adjust the spring tension (by bending the spring as required), check for evidence of discoloration. If the spring is blued or shows other obvious signs of overheating, plan on replacing it (since it has probably lost its temper).

And that's about it. If you do no more than check your brushes, wipe down the commutator, inspect all the mounting brackets, and check the drive belt (and pulleys) from time to time, you should be able to save yourself a little (maybe a lot of) money, downtime, and/or aggravation on generator maintenance over the next several hundred hours. You may even learn to *like* your generator.

GENERATOR TROUBLESHOOTING

Analyzing faulty generator functions calls for both a detailed knowledge of the system and logical acumen. In troubleshooting a Delco-Remy generator, here is how that would apply:

The Delco-Remy generator is of the two brush, shunt type and is controlled by a regulator operating on the principle of inserting resistance into the generator field circuit to cause a reduction of generator voltage and current output. With each generator is the regulator assembly, composed of a voltage regulator and current regulator, to prevent overloading of the battery and electrical circuits. Also with the regulator is a reverse current cutout to prevent the generator from being motorized by the battery when the generator output drops below the battery voltage. A paralleling relay is used on twin-engine aircraft to connect the two generators. The generator is usually located on the front lower right side of the engine and utilizes a belt drive from the engine crankshaft. The generator voltage regulator is located on the engine firewall. The best assurance of obtaining maximum service from the generator with minimum trouble is to follow a regular inspection and maintenance procedure, as we have just described.

Periodic lubrication where required, inspection of the brushes and commutator and checking of the brush spring tension are essentials in the inspection procedure. In addition, disassembly and thorough overhauling of the generator at periodic intervals are desirable as a safeguard against failures from accumulations of dust and grease and normal wear of parts. This is particularly desirable on installations where maintenance of operating schedules is of special importance. In addition to the generator itself, the external circuits between the generator, regulator and battery must be kept in good condition since defective wiring or loose or corroded connection will prevent normal generator and regulator action. At times, it may be necessary to adjust the voltage regulator, or if dual generators are installed, the voltage regulators and paralleling relay. See the section concluding this chapter for details on maintaining voltage regulators.

System Troubleshooting

In analyzing complaints of generator-regulator operation, any of several conditions may be found:

a. Fully charged battery and low charging rate: This indicates normal generator-regulator operation. Regulator setting may be checked as outlined below.

b. Fully charged battery and a high charging rate: This indicates that the voltage regulator is not reducing the generator output as it should. A high charging rate to a fully charged battery will damage the battery and the accompanying high voltage is very injurious to all electrical units. This operating condition may result from:

1. Improper voltage regulator setting.

2. Defective voltage regulator unit.

3. Grounded generator field circuit (in either generator, regulator or wiring).

4. Poor ground connections at regulator.

5. High temperature which reduces the resistance of the battery to charge so that it will accept a high charging rate even though the voltage regulator setting is normal.

If the trouble is not due to high temperature, determine the cause of trouble by disconnecting the lead from the regulator "F" terminal with the generator operating at medium speed. If the output remains high, the generator field is grounded either in the generator or in the wiring harness. If the output drops off, the regulator is at fault, and it should be checked for a high voltage setting or grounds.

c. Low battery and high charging rate: This is normal generator-regulator action. Regulator settings may be checked as outlined below.

d. Low battery and low or no charging rate: This condition could be due to:

1. Loose connections, frayed or damaged wires.

2. Defective battery.

3. High circuit resistance.

4. Low regulator setting.

5. Oxidized regulator contact points.

6. Defects within the generator.

If the condition is not caused by loose connections, frayed or damaged wires, proceed as follows to locate cause of trouble:

To determine whether the generator or regulator is at fault, momentarily ground the "F" terminal of the regulator and increase generator speed. If the output does not increase, the generator is probably at fault and should be checked as outlined further below. If the generator output increases, the trouble is due to:

1. A low voltage (or current) regulator setting.

2. Oxidized regulator contact points which insert excessive resistance into the generator field circuit so that output remains low.

3. Generator field circuit open within the regulator at the connections or in the regulator wiring.

e. Burned resistances, windings or contacts: These result from open circuit operation or high resistance in the charging circuit. Where burned resistances, windings or contacts are found, always check wiring before installing a new regulator. Otherwise the new regulator may also fail in the same way.

f. Burned relay contact points: this is due to reversed generator polarity. Generator polarity must be corrected as explained below after any checks of the regulator or generator, or after disconnecting and reconnecting leads.

No Output

If the generator will not produce any output, remove the cover band and check the commutator, brushes and internal connections. Sticking brushes, a dirty or gummy commutator, or poor connections may prevent the generator from producing any output. Thrown solder on the cover band indicates that the generator has been overloaded (allowed to produce excessive output) so it has overheated and melted the solder at the commutator riser bars. Solder thrown out often leads to an open circuit and burned commutator bars. If the brushes are satisfactorily seated and are making good contact with the commutator, and the cause of trouble is not apparent, use a set of test points and a test lamp as follows to locate the trouble (leads must be disconnected from generator terminals).

Raise the grounded brush from the commutator and insulate with a piece of cardboard. Check for grounds with test points from the generator main brush to the generator frame. If the lamp lights, it indicates that the generator is internally grounded. Location of the ground can be found by raising and insulating all brushes from the commutator and checking the brush holders, armature, commutator and field separately. Repair or replace defective parts as required.

NOTE: If a grounded field is found, check the regulator contact points, since a grounded field may have permitted an excessive field current which will have burned the regulator contact points. Burned regulator points should be cleaned or replaced as required.

If the generator is not grounded, check the field for an open circuit with a test lamp. The lamp should light when one test point is placed on the field terminal or grounded field lead and the other is placed on the brush holder to which the field is connected. If it does not light, the circuit is open. If the open is due to a broken lead or bad connection, it can be repaired, but if the open is inside one of the field coils, it must be replaced.

If the field is not open, check for a short circuit in the field by connecting a battery of the specified voltage and an ammeter in series with the field circuit. Proceed with care, since a shorted field may draw excessive current which might damage the ammeter. If the field is not within specification, new field coils will be required. (Refer to instructions below.)

NOTE: If a shorted field is found, check the regulator contact points, since a shorted field may have permitted excessive field current which would have caused the regulator contact points to burn. Clean or replace points as required.

If the trouble has not yet been located, check the armature for open and short circuits. Open circuits in the armature are usually obvious, since the open circuited commutator bars will arc every time they pass under the generator brushes so that they will soon become burned. If the bars are not too badly burned and the open circuit can be repaired, the armature can usually be saved. In addition to repairing the armature, generator output must be brought down to specifications to prevent overloading by readjustment of the regulator.

Short circuits in the armature are located by use of a growler. The armature is placed in the growler and slowly rotated (while a thin strip of steel such as a hacksaw blade is held above the armature core). The steel strip will vibrate above the area of the armature core in which short-circuited armature coils are located. If the short circuit is obvious, it can often be repaired so that the armature can be saved.

Unsteady or Low Output

If the generator produces a low or unsteady output, the following factors should be considered:

a. A loose drive belt will slip and cause a low or unsteady output.

b. Brushes which stick in their holders, or low brush spring tension will prevent good contact between the brushes and commutator so that output will be low and unsteady. This will also cause arcing and burning of the brushes and commutator.

c. If the commutator is dirty, out of round, or has high mica, generator output is apt to be low and unsteady. The remedy here is to turn the commutator down in a lathe and undercut the mica. Burned commutator bars may indicate an open circuit condition in the armature, as stated above.

Excessive Output

In a system which has the generator field circuit grounded externally, accidental internal grounding of the field circuit would prevent normal regulation so that excessive output might be produced by the generator. On this type of unit, an internally grounded field which would cause excessive output may be located by use of test points connected between the "F" terminal and the brush to which the field lead is connected inside the generator. The brush should be raised from the commutator before this test is made. If the lamp lights, the field is internally grounded. If the field has become grounded because the insulation on a field lead has worn away, repair can be made by reinsulating the lead. It is also possible to make repair where the ground has occurred at the pole shoes by removing the field coils and reinsulating and reinstalling them. A ground at the "F" terminal stud can be repaired by installing new washers or bushings.

NOTE: If battery temperature is excessive, battery overcharge is apt to occur, even though regulator settings are normal. Under this condition, it is permissible to reduce the voltage regulator setting as explained in the applicable bulletin pertaining to the regulator used on the application.

Noisy Generator

Noise emanating from a generator may be caused by a loose mounting, drive pulley, or gear; worn or dirty bearings; or improperly seated brushes. Dirty bearings may sometimes by saved by cleaning and relubrication, but worn bearings should be replaced. Brushes can be seated as explained earlier. If the brush holder is bent, it may be difficult to reseat the brush so that it will function properly without excessive noise. Such a brush holder will require replacement.

Field Coil Service

Field coils can be removed from the field frame most easily by use of a pole shoe screw driver. It is also advisable to use a pole shoe spreader, since this prevents distortion of the field frame. The pole shoe screw driver permits easy loosening and removal of the pole shoe screws so that the pole shoes and field coils can be taken out of the field frame. The pole shoe screw driver and spreader should be used on reassembly of the field frame. Careful reassembly is necessary to prevent shorting or grounding of the field coils as the pole shoes are tightened into place.

Grounded field coils may sometimes be repaired by removing them so they can be reinsulated. Care must be used to avoid excessive bulkiness when applying new isulation, since this might cause the pole shoe to cut through and cause another ground when the coils are reinstalled.

Usually if a field coil is open or shorted internally it will require replacement, since it is difficult to repair such a defect.

To remove or replace field coils in the field frame, the use of a pole shoe spreader and screw driver is recommended.

Armature Service

The armature should be checked for opens, shorts and grounds as explained in the following paragraphs. If the armature commutator is worn, dirty, out of round, or has high mica, the armature should be put in a lathe so the commutator can be turned down and the mica undercut. The mica should be undercut .031 of an inch and the slots cleaned out carefully to remove any trace of dirt or copper dust. As a final step in this procedure, the commutator should be sanded lightly with No. 00 sandpaper to remove any slight burrs that might be left as a result of the undercutting procedures.

Special Note: The armature or field coil should not be cleaned in any degreasing tank or by use of degreasing compounds, since this might damage insulation so that a short or ground would subsequently develope. Sealed ball bearings do not require cleaning or

relubrication. Other generator parts should be cleaned and carefully inspected for wear and other damage. Any defective parts should be repaired or replaced. On reassembly all soldered electrical connections should be made with rosin flux. Acid flux must never be used on electrical connections.

Open circuited armatures can often be saved when the open is obvious and repairable. The most likely place an open will occur is at the commutator riser bars. This usually results from overloading of the generator which causes overheating and melting of the solder. Repair can be effected by resoldering the leads in the riser bars (using rosin flux) and turning down the commutator in a lathe to remove the burned spot and then undercutting the mica as explained in the previous paragraph. In some heavy-duty armatures, the leads are welded into the riser bars and these cannot be repaired by resoldering.

Short circuits in the armature are located by use of a growler. When the armature is revolved in the growler, with a steel strip such as a hacksaw blade held above it, the blade will vibrate above the area of the armature core in which the short is located. Copper or brush dust in the slots between the commutator bars sometimes causes shorts between bars which can be eliminated by cleaning out the slots. Shorts at cross-overs of the coils at the core end can often be eliminated by bending wires slightly and reinsulating the exposed bare wire.

Grounds in the armature are detected by use of a test lamp and test points. If the lamp lights when one test point is placed on the commutator with the other point on the core or shaft, the armature is grounded. Grounds occur as a result of insulation failure, which is often brought on by overloading and consequent overheating of the generator. Repairs can sometimes be made if grounds are at core ends (where coils come out of slots) by placing insulating strips between the core and coil which has grounded.

Repolarizing the Generator

After a generator has been repaired and reinstalled or at any time after a generator has been tested, it must be repolarized to make sure that it has the correct polarity with respect to the battery it is to charge. Failure to repolarize the generator may result in burned relay contact points, a run-down battery and possibly serious damage to the generator itself. The procedure to follow in correcting generator polarity depends upon the generator-regulator wiring circuits; that is, whether the generator field is internally grounded or is grounded through the regulator.

HOW TO INSPECT AND MAINTAIN A VOLTAGE REGULATOR

Airplane charging systems have undergone a steady evolution over the years, with alternators supplanting old-style generators on most general aviation planes beginning around 1968, and 24-volt systems largely replacing 12-volt systems beginning in 1978 (Mooney excepted). Along the way, voltage regulation—like everything else— has gone solid-state, with a Zener diode and a couple of transistors (integral to the alternator in most cases) doing the work of two or three cantankerous relays.

Even so, a good many operators of older aircraft are still flying around with old-style (mechanical, not solid-state) voltage regulators—the kind that require periodic point adjustment, contact dressing, and screwdriver tweaking (actual maintenance, in other words) to perform reliably.

The typical regulator consists of a cutout relay, a voltage regulator and a current regulator unit. The cutout relay closes the generator to battery circuit when the generator voltage is sufficient to charge the battery, and it opens the circuit when the generator slows down or stops. The voltage regulator unit is a voltage-limiting device that prevents the system voltage from exceeding a specified maximum and thus protects the battery and other voltage-sensitive equipment. The current regulator unit is a current-limiting device that limits the generator output so as not to exceed its rated maximum.

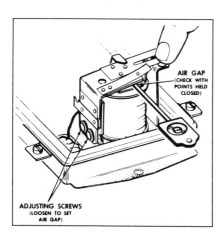

Checking and adjusting relay air gap.

The Cutout Relay

The cutout relay has two windings, a series winding of a few turns of heavy copper wire and a shunt winding of many turns of fine copper wire. The shunt winding is connected across the generator so that generator voltage is impressed upon it at all times. The series winding is connected in series with the charging circuit so that all generator output passes through it. The relay core and windings are assembled into a frame. A flat steel armature is attached to the frame by a flexible hinge so that it is centered just above the stationary contact points. When the generator is not operating, the armature contact points are held away from the stationary points by the tension of a flat spring riveted on the side of the armature.

When the generator voltage builds up a value great enough to charge the battery, the magnetism induced by the relay windings is sufficient to pull the armature toward the core so that the contact points close. This completes the circuit between the generator and battery. The current which flows from the generator to the battery passes through the series winding in a direction to add to the magnetism holding the armature down and the contact points closed.

When the generator slows down or stops, current begins to flow from the battery to the generator.

This reverse flow of current through the series winding causes a reversal of the series winding magnetic field. The magnetic field of the shunt winding does not reverse. Therefore, instead of helping each other, the two windings now oppose so that the resultant magnetic field becomes insufficient to hold the armature down. The flat spring pulls the armature away from the core so that the points separate; this opens the circuit between the generator and battery.

The Voltage Regulator

The voltage regulator has two windings assembled on a single core, including both a shunt winding consisting of many turns of fine copper wire which is shunted across the generator, and a series winding of a few turns of relatively heavy copper wire which is connected in series with the generator field circuit when the regulator contact points are closed.

The windings and core are assembled into a frame. A flat steel armature is attached to the frame by a flexible hinge so that it is just above the end of the core. The armature contains a contact point which is just beneath a stationary contact point. When the voltage regulator is not operating, the tension of a spiral spring holds the armature away from the core so that the points are in contact and the generator field circuit is completed to ground through them.

UPPER ARMATURE STOP
(BEND TO ADJUST POINT
OPENING)

POINT
OPENING

Checking and adjusting relay point opening.

When the generator voltage reaches the value for which the voltage regulator is adjusted, the magnetic field produced by the two windings (shunt and series) overcomes the armature spring tension and pulls the armature down so that the contact points separate. This inserts resistance into the generator field circuit so that the generator field current and voltage are reduced. Reduction of the generator voltage reduces the magnetic field of the regulator shunt winding. Also, opening the regulator points opens the regulator series winding circuit so that its magnetic field collapses completely. The consequence is that the magnetic field is reduced sufficiently to allow the spiral spring to pull the armature away from the core so that the contact points again close. This directly grounds the generator so that generator voltage and output increase. The above cycle of action again takes place, and the cycle continues at a rate of 50 to 200 times a second, regulating the voltage to a predetermined value. With the voltage thus limited, the generator supplies varying amounts of current to meet the varying states of battery charge and electrical load.

The Current Regulator

The current regulator has a series winding of a few turns of heavy wire which carries all generator output. The winding core is assembled into a frame. A flat steel armature is attached to the frame by a flexible hinge so that it is just above the core. The armature has a contact point which is just below a stationary contact point. When the current regulator is not operating, the tension of a spiral spring holds the armature away from the core so that the points are in contact. In this position the generator field circuit is completed to ground through the current regulator contact points in series with the voltage regulator contact points.

When the load demands are heavy, as for example, when electrical devices are turned on and the battery is in a discharged condition, the voltage may not increase to a value sufficient to cause the voltage regulator to operate. Consequently, generator output will continue to increase until the generator reaches rated maximum current. This is the current value for which the current regulator is set. Therfore, when the generator reaches rated output, this output, flowing through the current regulator winding, creates sufficient magnetism to pull the current regulator armature down and open the contact points. With the points open, resistance is inserted into the generator field circuit so that the generator output is reduced.

As soon as the generator output starts to fall off, the magnetic field of the current regulator winding is reduced, the spiral spring tension pulls the armature up, the contact points close and directly connect the generator field to ground. Output increases and the above cycle is repeated. The cycle continues to take place while the current regulator is in operation 50 to 200 times a second, preventing the generator from exceeding its rated maximum. When the electrical load is reduced (electrical devices turned off or battery comes up to charge), then the voltage increases so that the voltage regulator begins to operate and tapers the generator output down. This prevents the current regulator from operating. Either the voltage regulator or the current regulator operates at any one time—the two do not operate at the same time.

Resistances

The current and voltage regulator circuits use a common resistor which is inserted in the field circuit when either the current or voltage regulator operates. A second resistor often is connected between the regulator field terminal and the cutout relay frame, which places it in parallel with the generator field coils. The sudden reduction in field current occurring when the current or voltage regulator contact points open, is accompanied by a surge of induced voltage in the field coils as the strength of the magnetic field changes. These surges are partially dissipated by the two resistors, thus preventing excessive arcing at the contact points.

Temperature Compensation

Voltage regulators are compensated for temperature by means of a bimetal thermostatic hinge on the armature. This causes the regulator to regulate at a higher voltage when cold, which partly compensates for the fact that a higher voltage is required to charge a cold battery. Many current regulators also have a bimetal thermostatic hinge on the

Delco-Remy Regulator Specifications (Piper Aztec)			
Regulator Model	1119246[1]	1118976[1]	1119656[2]
Delco-Remy Ref. Serv. Bulletin	1R-116A	1R-116	1R-119A
Cutout Relay:			
Air Gap	0.020 in.	0.017 in.	0.017 in.
Point Opening	0.020 in.	0.032 in.	0.032 in.
Closing Voltage	11.8-13.5 volts	24-27 volts	22.8-25.2 volts
Voltage Regulator:			
Air Gap	0.075 in.	0.075 in.	0.067 in.
Current Setting	65°F - 14.2-15.7 volts 85°F - 14.4-15.4 volts 105°F - 14.2-15.0 volts	27.9-29.4 volts	65°F - 29.4-31.4 volts[3] 85°F - 28.9-30.8 volts[3] 105°F - 28.3-30.1 volts[3]
Current Regulator:			
Air Gap	0.075 in.	0.075 in.	0.075 in.
Current Setting	48-52 amps	23-27 amps	48-52 amps

[1] Paralleling: With no load on battery terminal, add 5-amp load at P-terminal—voltage regulator to operate 2 to 3 volts lower.

[2] Paralleling: With no load on battery terminal, add 2.5-amp load at P-terminal—voltage regulator to operate 2 to 3 volts lower.

[3] Operation on lower contacts must be 0.2 to 0.6 volts lower than on upper contacts.

armature. This permits a somewhat higher generator output when the unit is cold, but causes the output to drop off as temperature increases.

Regulator Polarity

Some regulators are designed for use with negative grounded systems, while other regulators are designed for use with positive grounded systems. Using the wrong polarity regulator on an installation will cause the regulator contact points to pit badly and give short life. As a safeguard against installation of the wrong polarity regulator, all regulators of this type have the model number and the polarity clearly stamped on the end of the regulator base.

Maintenance: General Precautions

Mechanical checks and adjustments (air gaps, point opening) must be made with battery disconnected and regulator preferably off the aircraft. Caution: The cutout relay contact points must never be closed by hand with the battery connected to the regulator. This would cause a high current to flow through the units which would seriously damage them.

Electrical checks and adjustments may be made either on or off the airplane. The regulator must always be operated with the type of generator for which it is designed.

The regulator must be mounted in the operating position when electrical settings are checked and adjusted and it must be at operating temperature.

During testing, generators must be operated at a speed sufficient to produce current in excess of specified setting. Voltage of the generator must be kept high enough to insure sufficient current output, but below the operating voltage of the voltage regulator unit.

After any tests or adjustments the generator on the airplane must be polarized after the leads are connected, but before the engine is started, as follows: After reconnecting the leads, momentarily connect a jumper lead between the GEN and BAT terminals of the regulator. This allows a momentary surge of current to flow through the generator, which correctly polarizes it. Failure to do this may result in severe damage to the equipment since reversed polarity causes vibration, arcing and burning of the relay contact points.

Cleaning Contact Points

The contact points of a regulator will not operate indefinitely without some attention. It has been found that a great majority of all regulator trouble can be eliminated by a simple cleaning of the contact points, plus some possible readjustment. The flat points should be cleaned with a spoon or riffler file. On negative grounded regulators which have the flat contact point on the regulator armatures, loosen the contact bracket mounting screws so that the bracket can be tilted to one side. A flat file cannot be used successfully to clean the flat contact points since it will not touch the center of the flat point where point wear is most apt to occur. Never use emery cloth or sandpaper to clean the contact points. Remove all the oxides from the contact points but note that it is not necessary to remove any cavity that may have developed.

Voltage Regulator Setting

Two checks and adjustments are required on the voltage regulator; air gap and voltage setting.

a. Air Gap: To check the air gap, push the armature down until the contact points are just touching and then measure the air gap. Adjust by loosening the contact mounting screws and raising or lowering the contact bracket as required. Be sure the points are lined up and tighten the screws after adjustment.

b. Voltage Setting: There are two ways to check the voltage setting; the fixed resistance method and the variable resistance method.

1. Fixed Resistance Method:

(a) Connect a fixed resistance between the battery terminal and ground after disconnecting the battery lead from the battery terminal of the regulator. The resistance must be one and one-half ohms for 14-·volt and seven ohms for 28-volt units. It must be capable of carrying 10 amperes without any change of resistance with temperature changes.

(b) Connect a voltmeter from the regulator BAT terminal to ground.

(c) Place a thermometer within 0.25 inch of regulator cover to measure the regulator ambient temperature.

(d) Operate the generator at specified speed for 15 minutes with the regulator cover in place to bring the voltage regulator to operating temperature.

(e) Cycle the generator:

Method 1: Move the voltmeter lead from BAT to GEN terminal of the regulator. Retard generator speed until generator voltage is reduced to 4 volts. Move the voltmeter lead back to the BAT terminal of the regulator. Bring the generator back to specified speed and note the voltage setting.

Method 2: Connect a variable resistance into the field circuit. Turn out all resistance. Operate the generator at specified speed. Slowly increase (turn in) resistance until generator voltage is reduced to 4 volts. Turn out all resistance again and note the voltage setting (with the voltmeter connected). The regulator cover must be in place.

(f) Note the thermometer reading and select the normal range of voltage for this temperature as listed in the accompanying specifications table.

(g) Note the voltmeter reading with the regulator cover in place.

(h) To adjust the voltage setting, turn the adjusting screw. Turn clockwise to increase the setting and counterclockwise to decrease the setting.

CAUTION: If the adjusting screw is turned down (clockwise) beyond range, spring support may not return when the screw is backed off. In such case, turn the screw counterclockwise until there is ample clearance between the screw head and spring support. Then bend the spring support up carefully until it touches the screw head. Final setting of the unit should always be made by increasing spring tension, never by reducing it. If the setting is too high, adjust the unit below the required value and then raise to the exact setting by increasing the spring tension. After each adjustment and before taking a reading, replace the regulator cover and cycle the generator.

2. Variable Resistance Method:

(a) Connect an ammeter and a one-quarter ohm variable resistor in series with the battery.

NOTE: It is very important that the variable resistance be connected at the BAT terminal rather than at the GEN terminal even though these terminals are in the same circuit.

(b) Connect the voltmeter between the BAT terminal and ground.

(c) Place a thermometer within one-quarter inch of the regulator cover to measure the regulator ambient temperature.

(d) Operate the generator at specified speed. Adjust the variable resistor until the current flow is 8 to 10 amperes. If less current than is required above is flowing, it will be necessary to turn on the airplane lights to permit increased generator output. Variable resistance can then be used to decrease the current flow to the required amount.

Allow the generator to operate at this speed and current flow for 15 minutes with the regulator cover in place in order to bring the voltage regulator to operating temperature.

(e) Cycle the generator by either method listed in the "Fixed Resistance Method" procedure.

(f) Note the thermometer reading and select the "normal range" of voltage for this temperature as listed in the specifications table.

(g) Note the voltmeter reading with the regulator cover in place.

(h) Adjust the voltage regulator as required as described in step (h) of the "Fixed Resistance Method" procedure. In using the variable resistance method, it is necessary to readjust the variable resistance after each voltage adjustment to assure that 8 to 10 amperes are flowing. Cycle the generator after each adjustment before reading the voltage regulator setting with the cover in place.

Chapter 6

BATTERIES

If alternators and generators are inconveniently vulnerable to injury, aircraft batteries often seem downright wimpish and sickly. Unless they are adequately maintained and pampered, they can leave us on the ramp with tens or hundreds of thousands of dollars' worth of aircraft that is not about to go anywhere without outside help. A variation on the theme is being left high in cloud with the alternator or generator gone south and a battery all too soon heading in the same direction as it dribbles out a last, small measure of power. As we shall see, the ills that batteries are heir to stem from the laws of chemistry, the effects of heat and cold, and the insults of human neglect. Fortunately, rational and regular maintenance can do much to prolong a battery's life and thus reduce more than one kind of cost.

BASIC MAINTENANCE PROCEDURES

Unfortunately, since the average aircraft owner doesn't even check the tires of his airplane with a gauge once a month, he is not likely to

remove the battery frequently for servicing. Yet most airframe and battery manufacturers strongly recommend that aircraft batteries be removed for rejuvenation at least every 30 days.

The Beech Model 35 *Shop Manual* is typical of most airframe manufacturers' service publications in its "Battery Maintenance Program" recommendations. According to Beech, the aircraft battery should be removed from the airplane for service every 30 days under normal conditions. Furthermore, "if the ambient temperatures are above 90°F or the time between engine starts averages less than 30 minutes, *the time between servicings should be reduced.*" In other words, in hot weather—or any time short hops are repeatedly made—servicing the battery once a month is not enough. Instead, you should actually check out the battery once every other week, or even once every 10 days. Or oftener.

If you're not already doing your own battery checks (and battery recharging, and—when necessary—battery replacement) yourself, you ought to start doing so now. Not just to save money on hired-out maintenance (although you will), but to keep your battery in constant tip-top shape (thereby prolonging its life), and to give yourself peace of mind.

The alternative? Neglect your battery (i.e., let someone else check it on a catch-as-catch-can basis), and buy a new one every 18 months. It's as simple as that.

The 30-Day Check

Contrary to what you may have been led to believe, aircraft lead-acid batteries are really not much different from automotive lead-acid batteries. They're somewhat smaller (which accounts for their lower amp-hour ratings), their posts are designed somewhat differently (to accept wing nuts), and they have spill-proof vent caps (to prevent acid leakage during severe turbulence), but the chemistry, the cell voltages, and the construction methods used in aviation batteries are virtually the same as those used for automotive batteries. Which, in turn, means that the basic maintenance requirements for the two battery types are the same.

In general, routine servicing of an aircraft lead-acid battery consists of adding water to the cells as needed, ascertaining the state of charge of the battery, and cleaning up any corrosion that may have accumulated in the vicinity of the battery box. These are the operations which

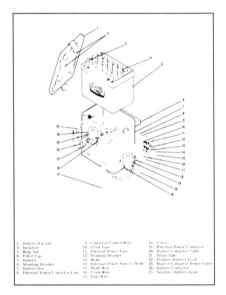

1. Battery Box Lid
2. Insulator
3. Wing Nut
4. Filler Cap
5. Battery
6. Mounting Bracket
7. Battery Box
8. External Power Contactor Line
9. Contactor Control Wire
10. Clock Fuse
11. External Power Fuse
12. Mounting Bracket
13. Diode
14. External Power Fuse to Diode
15. Diode Wire
16. Clock Wire
17. Fuse Wire
18. Cover
19. External Power Contactor
20. Starter Contactor Cable
21. Drain Tube
22. Positive Battery Lead
23. Starter Contactor Power Cable
24. Battery Contactor
25. Negative Battery Lead

Removing the battery is usually easy enough when the battery box is accessible. In a fairly typical Cessna single, it will be found on the firewall, near the battery and external power contactors.

Beech (and practically all other airframe manufacturers) recommends be performed every 30 days, or more often in hot weather.

FIRST, A NOTE OF CAUTION: Aircraft battery electrolyte contains 30 percent sulfuric acid. Observe proper safety precautions when working around any lead-acid battery. Serious burns may result if acid is not immediately flushed from the skin or eyes with copious amounts of water. For optimum protection, wear gloves and eye protectors. Neutralize spills immediately with baking soda.

To measure the charge level of your battery, you will, of course, need a *battery hydrometer*. This device will enable you to determine the *specific gravity* of the electrolyte in the battery's cells. (The higher the concentration of sulfuric acid in the electrolyte, the higher the solution's density—and the greater the state of charge of the battery. For a fully charged battery, the electrolyte will have a specific gravity of about 1.300—which simply means the electrolyte is 1.3 times as dense as pure water.) The reason you can't simply measure the battery's voltage with a voltmeter to determine the state of charge is that a lead-acid battery's open-circuit voltage remains fairly constant throughout a wide range of charge levels.

If you don't already have a battery hydrometer for your plane, get one now. (You'll find that it comes in handy for adding water to the battery, as well as for checking charge.) And yes, despite what anyone may have told you, you *can* use an automotive battery hydrometer. The so-called "aircraft battery hydrometers" sold by the various pilots' supply houses are simply scaled-down car-battery testers—scaled down because [1] aircraft batteries are often located in cramped quarters, and [2] many of the larger hydrometers on the automotive market require more electrolyte per sampling than an aircraft battery's tiny cells can provide.

When you go shopping for a hydrometer, look for a fairly compact model (i.e., stay away from those giant "calf feeders" that you see so often at auto parts stores)—and be sure the tool you buy has a numerical scale. You don't want one of those 99-cent jobs that simply register "battery good" and "needs recharging."

Whether or not you decide to take the battery out of the plane before servicing it will depend, to a large extent, on how conveniently located the unit is. Unlike automobile batteries—which are generally quite accessible—aircraft batteries are often hidden in remote parts of the airframe, which probably accounts for the neglect that most plane batteries receive at the hands of their owners. In some airplanes (Cessna 150s and 172s, for instance), the battery is firewall-mounted; in others (many Cherokees, Cessna 182s, etc.) the battery is located aft of the cockpit; in still others (Piper Warriors, for example), the battery may be located beneath a passenger seat. In all cases, the battery is enclosed in a protective container which is vented (by means of a tube) to the outside of the airframe.

If your battery is fairly easily reached, you may wish to service it in the plane (as mentioned before); otherwise, you should remove it. Taking the battery out isn't as hard as you might think. First, you'll need to unclip (or otherwise remove) the top of the battery box and lay

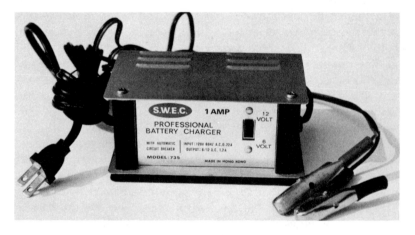

The S.W.E.C. Model 735 charger is very inexpensive (but UL listed) and charges at a modest 1 amp rate—generally good for home charging.

The Schauer K324 charges 24-volt batteries and does so with a tapering charge rate, beginning nominally at 3 amperes.

it aside or—if the lid is wet—remove it from the aircraft. Next, determine which of the battery posts is the negative post, and loosen the wing nut on that terminal. Temporarily remove the wing nut, lift the lead wire for that terminal off the post, and replace the nut. As a precautionary measure, place a piece of masking tape over the end of the negative lead wire.

Now repeat the foregoing steps with the battery's positive post. Then grab the little rope handle atop the battery and (deep breath) hoist the battery up out of its container. It's the hardest part of removing a battery from any airplane—physically lifting it from its box.

VERY IMPORTANT: Do not vary from the above procedure. All aircraft batteries are negatively grounded, which means that—for the danger of sparking (and explosion) to be minimized—it is necessary to disconnect the *negative* battery lead *first*. Likewise, when reinstalling the serviced battery, connect the negative lead wire *last*.

What to Check

After removing the battery from the plane, give it a thorough examination for damage. Among other things, look for cracks in the rubber case, loose posts, and severe corrosion damage. Wetness on the top of the case and the filler caps can either mean that someone overfilled the battery with water, or the battery is being charged too

Table 1

Specific Gravity vs. Charge Level

Hydrometer Reading	State of Charge
1.280	100%
1.250	75%
1.220	50%
1.190	25%
1.160	(dead)

Note: The information given is for an electrolyte temperature of 80°F. To correct for temperature variations, refer to Table 2.

rapidly. Wipe up any liquid with a sponge, preferably after sprinkling baking soda on the affected area. (Be careful not to let any soda enter the filler caps, or damage to the battery's cells will result.)

Incidentally, if you happened to notice a sticky goo on the battery's posts (and perhaps also on the top of the battery), don't be alarmed. The battery is not melting. The goo is petroleum jelly, applied as a preservative by whoever last serviced the battery.

If your battery is an Exide AC-78M or a Willard W-78 M, check it to see whether the code markings N-8, A-9 or B-9 appear on either terminal post. The presence of one of these code markings means that your battery is affected by AD 79-07-02, which states that the battery must be permanently removed from service "before next flight."

Now (before you add water) is the time to check electrolyte specific gravity, if you are going to. Take a sample of fluid from a cell with your hydrometer (start with a clean hydrometer; wash it, if necessary) and compare the specific gravity reading you get with the values shown in Table 1.

Note that the numbers shown in Table 1 are only valid for an electrolyte temperature of 80°F. If the temperature is higher or lower than this (you can estimate the temperature difference, or measure it with an inexpensive darkroom thermometer), you'll need to add or subtract points as shown in Table 2 to correct the specific gravity reading.

At normal ambient air temperatures, during normal battery servicing, the effect of temperature on electrolyte specific gravity will not be significant. Where this effect becomes important is during charging operations, when battery temperatures can go as high as 120°F, 130°F, or higher, Here, it is important that you have (and use) a thermometer, and correct your hydrometer readings according to Table 2.

If your battery has seen heavy service or is more than a year old, it would be a good idea at this point to check the charge level of all six (or all twelve, for a 24-volt battery) cells, and compare specific readings. According to the FAA's bible on aircraft inspection and repair

Table 2		
Specific Gravity Temperature Correction		
Electrolyte temperature		Amount to be added to
°F	°C	specific gravity
140	60	+.024
130	55	+.020
120	49	+.016
110	43	+.012
100	38	+.008
90	33	+.004
80	27	0
70	21	-.004
60	15	-.008
50	10	-.016
40	5	-.020
30	-2	-.024
20	-7	-.028
10	-13	-.032
0	-18	-.036
-10	-23	-.040

For example: If electrolyte gives a specific gravity reading of 1.200 at 100°F, the corrected reading (for 80° conditions) is 1.200 plus .008 or 1.208.

(AC43. 13-1A), "When a specific gravity difference of 0.050 or more exists between cells of a battery, the battery is approaching the end of its useful life and replacement should be considered." For your specific gravity comparisons to be meaningful, the battery should be at or near full charge.

If necessary, put the battery on a charger (more about that shortly) and recheck the cells.

After you have checked the charge level of the battery (but not before), add water to each cell as necessary to bring the electrolyte level about 3/8 of an inch above the tops of the plates.

Distilled water is best, but any odorless, tasteless water may be added. Do not add more water than necessary; the slightest excess will be expelled out the vent caps, leading to potential corrosion problems.

Speaking of corrosion problems, be sure to check your airframe (or firewall) in the vicinity of the battery box for corrosion before reinstalling the serviced battery. Corrosion detection is one of the more important reasons for servicing your battery every 30 days; what may have been a clean battery area last month could well be a pocket of severe corrosion now.

If you find any corrosion, neutralize the area with baking soda, flush with water, and blow dry with compressed air.

Alumimum should be cleaned down to the bare metal either with aluminum wool, or a moist sponge and a non-chlorinated household cleaner such as Bon-Ami.

Steel can, of course, be cleaned up with steel wool. In any case, be sure to flush the entire area with clean water and blow dry when clean-up operations are concluded.

Examine the area where the battery vent tube exits the plane and—if necessary—remove all traces of corrosion. Also, check to be sure the vent tube is unobstructed.

In some aircraft, the battery vent line connects to a jar containing a piece of felt saturated with a strong bicarbonate solution. If you find such a jar, remove and rinse out the felt pad, then soak it in a solution made by dissolving one pound of baking soda in one gallon of water. Replace the pad.

Battery Charging Made Simple

Any time you find that your battery electrolyte has a specific gravity of less than 1.22 (50 percent charge), you should put the unit on a charger before putting it back in service. As a rule, batteries come to need charging for one of two reasons: Either the battery has been run down through overuse, or it actually has been allowed to see long periods of *disuse.*

The two most popular ways to run an aircraft battery down seem to be to leave the master switch on overnight and to crank a hard-starting engine until it won't crank any more. Offhand, one wouldn't think that (with all lights and radios off) leaving a master switch on for ten or twenty hours would cause a battery to go dead; but, in fact, the current drawn by all the things that are on when the master is on (the battery contactor, alternator field windings, electric gyro motors, fuel and cylinder temp gauges, etc.) seldom amounts to less than a full amp, and a one-amp drain over a period of 24 hours will certainly run a battery down.

Prolonged engine cranking isn't *good* for batteries, but it should be noted that (unlike a battery that has been discharged by a long-term one-amp drain) a battery whose charge has been depleted by five minutes of heavy cranking (involving loads of up to 150 amps) may actually come back up by itself if allowed to rest a few minutes. That's because during periods of extremely heavy demand, the outsides of the cell plates will become discharged very quickly, while the material on the *inside* of the plates remains in good condition.

Give the battery a chance to rest (i.e., give the plate material time to migrate from the inside to the surface), and you may well find—if the battery did not sustain heat-related internal injuries during the previous cranking episode—that the charge level will come up enough to crank the engine some more, although, obviously, if you have to do

Overcharging can boil the electrolyte and expose the plates, as in this battery.

this much cranking, something is seriously wrong and further starting attempts should be postponed until the problem (whatever it is) is corrected.

Regardless of how the battery got run down, a weakened battery should be placed on a charger in accordance with the manufacturer's instructions. Usually, charging instructions are printed (or molded) on the battery somewhere. The Rebat model R-35, for instance, contains the following words molded into the side of the case:

FULLY CHARGED SP. GR. 1.270
RECHARGE REQUIRED WHEN SP. GR.REACHES 1.225
START CHG. 4 AMP—FINISH CHG. 2 AMP
MAXIMUM TEMPERATURE ON CHARGE 120°F

If no instructions are given on your battery, start with a charging current equal to 7 percent of the battery's ampere-hour rating. In other words, if you have a 25-amp-hour battery, do not apply more than 1.75 amps of current during charging.

Battery chargers are not expensive, so if you intend to do much of your own battery maintenance you definitely should invest in one. J.C. Whitney (P.O. Box 8410, Chicago, IL 60680) offers a UL-listed, 1.2-amp 12-volt battery charger with overcurrent protector for less than ten dollars. For a little more, you can go all out and get a taper-rate 6-

amp charger with built-in ammeter and self-resetting circuit-breakers (again from J.C. Whitney). The latter type of charger begins at a high current and automatically adjusts the rate of charge downward through a period of several hours.

How long should you leave your battery on the charger? The charge time will vary, depending on how badly discharged the battery was to begin with, how much charging current is used, and how hot or cold the battery (and surrounding air) is. In general, an aircraft battery is assumed to be fully charged when three consecutive hydrometer readings taken an hour apart show no change in specific gravity. (Note: Do *not* leave a fully charged battery on the charger any longer than necessary. Overcharging will damage the battery.)

So far, we have been talking only about recharging batteries that have been discharged through heavy (or continuous light) use. The charging procedure for a battery that has gone dead through *lack* of use is somewhat different. When a battery is allowed to sit unused and un-recharged for a period of days or weeks, a phenomenon known as *sulfation* occurs. That is simply where the lead sulfate that forms on the cells' plates as the battery slowly and spontaneously discharges (through normal self-discharging) combines with the lead sulfate that is present to a greater or lesser degree on the plates of *all* batteries (the exact degree depending on the state of the charge) to form a hard crust. This crust tends to insulate the plate material; in time, it may become so thick that no amount of recharging will dislodge it.

When you climb into your plane's cockpit after a month's absence and turn on your master switch only to find that the battery is dead, sulfation is usually the culprit. (Not always, though. Sometimes it's a bad battery contactor—the little relay that connects the battery to the rest of the electrical system when the master is turned on.) Here, the standard procedure is to take the battery out of the plane and charge it at half the factory-recommended charge current for 50 to 100 hours. Generally speaking, if this doesn't restore the battery's health, nothing will, and you can throw the battery away.

No matter what the recharging technique being used—and no matter whether the battery is sulfated, fully discharged, or merely feeling a little low—the following rules should always be observed, in the interests of safety:

[1] Remove the battery from the aircraft and place it in a well-ventilated area. Whenever a battery is recharged, explosive gases (oxygen and hydrogen) are produced in significant quantities. These

gases should not be allowed to collect in engine compartments, tailcones, small rooms, etc.

[2] To reduce the chance of spark formation, be sure the charger is OFF whenever you connect or disconnect the battery. Likewise, when the battery is charging, do not smoke or create other fire hazards.

[3] Loosen the battery's vent caps to facilitate the release of gas.

[4] Periodically check the specific gravity of the cells' electrolyte to determine when charging should be discontinued.

[5] Do not allow gassing cells to boil dry; check the cells' fluid level from time to time and add water as needed.

[6] Monitor the battery's temperature and do not let it exceed 120°F (extremely warm to the touch). Decrease the charging current and/or temporarily discontinue charging if this temperature limit is approached.

[7] *Always follow the manufacturer's instructions, in addition to (or in spite of) the instructions given here.*

REPLACEMENT AND PRESERVATION

Saving money on battery maintenance is largely a matter of [1] seeing to it that the battery is serviced at regular intervals (so that it will not die prematurely due to sulfation, dehydration, etc.), and [2] doing all the servicing yourself, rather than paying someone else—perhaps someone who stands to make a buck if you should suddenly need to buy a battery—to do the servicing for you.

Saving money on battery maintenance is *also* largely a matter of knowing how to buy replacement batteries cheaply; knowing how to charge and install new batteries yourself; and knowing how to operate a replacement battery in such a way that it lives to a ripe old age (perhaps three, even four years). Few pilots really understand how to do any of these things. Let's examine each of these areas one by one.

How You Can Save Money on New Batteries

The first thing to understand about choosing a replacement battery for your aircraft is that you do not need to buy the same make and model of battery that originally came with the plane. The fact that your plane has, say, a Gill battery in it now does not mean you can't go out and buy a Rebat or an Exide (or some other kind of) replacement.

The second thing you should know about buying batteries is that you are not limited to the Big Three aviation brands—Exide, Gill, and

Rebat—in choosing a replacement for your present battery. (In fact, if your goal is to spend the least amount of money possible on a new battery, you'll do well to *avoid* these particular brands). It turns out there are many "minor" makes and models of aircraft batteries to choose from—all (or almost all) of them perfectly legal for use in most planes.

How, exactly, can you tell whether a particular battery is right for your plane? Amazingly, there are no FAA guidelines in this department. Unlike autopilots, brakes, vacuum pumps, and other accessories, batteries carry no Supplemental Type Certificate approval for installation in various models of planes. There is no TSO for batteries. Nor are aircraft batteries manufactured under PMA approval. According to Gene Sherman, of the Office of General Aviation, FAA headquarters, Washington, D.C.: "The only rule governing the installation of lead-acid batteries in aircraft is that which says that an airplane must—upon completion of any maintenance—be in its original or properly altered condition." (The rule is FAR 43.13.)

"The FAA does not monitor the manufacture of aircraft batteries," Sherman says,"which means it is up to the owner-operator to ensure that the battery in his plane is of a type equal to or better than the original battery which was in the plane when it received its type certification." In effect, this means that a replacement battery must be of aircraft-style construction (i.e., it must have spill-proof vent caps), it must be approximately the same size and weight as the original battery, and its capacity (in amp-hours) must be equal to or more than that of the original. "If the replacement battery is heavier than the original one, or if modifications must be made to the battery box," Sherman adds, "then, of course, STC approval must be obtained prior to installation."

Because there is no TSO for lead-acid batteries, and because no form of type certification or Parts Manufacturer Approval is required of aircraft battery manufacturers, the number of companies offering aircraft batteries is high, and prices are relatively competitive.

When to Buy a New Battery

The time to buy a new battery is not when your old one wears out (i.e., when it goes dead and can't be recharged), but right now.

There are several reasons for this. First, battery prices may rise. (The manufacture of batteries in an energy-intensive process. Also, the polypropylene of which battery cases are made is derived from petroleum.)

Another factor to consider is that if you wait until your present battery conks out to buy a new one, you probably won't want to ground your plane for the two to three weeks it takes to obtain a discount battery by mail. Given a choice of waiting three weeks for a new battery to arrive, or buying a battery from your local FBO (thus eliminating downtime), you'll probably go the FBO route and end up paying full list price for a Gill, Rebat, or Exide battery (which is all that most dealers stock).

If you want to save money—and downtime—you'll write out a check for your next battery this week. It's as simple as that.

How to Activate a Dry-Charged Battery

New aircraft batteries are sold in the *dry-charged state* (i.e., minus electrolyte)—which means that before you can install one in your plane, you'll have to activate it according to the instructions that come with the battery.

Dry-charged batteries and battery electrolyte should be stored in a cool and dry place with ambient temperature between 60 and 90 degrees Fahrenheit.

Generally, you'll start by removing the vent caps and eliminating any sealing device that may have been used to seal the vent openings. Next, you'll trundle on down to your local service station and ask to buy some battery electrolyte (the instructions with the battery will tell you the recommended specific gravity to use); mail-order suppliers are prohibited from shipping electrolyte by mail. You'll need about a quart and a half of electrolyte to fill a standard 12-volt, 25-amp-hour aircraft battery or a little over two quarts for a standard 12-volt, 35-amp-hour battery. Bring the fluid level just above the tops of the plates and separators; do not overfill the cells. Gently rock the battery from side to side to help trapped air escape.

At this point, you'll need to give the battery a *boost charge* (a short-duration, high-current charge) to activate it. Ask the service attendant (or your FBO) if you can put your battery on the shop's charger for 10 minutes. Charge the battery at 15 amps for 10 minutes (or as stated on the instruction sheet with the battery).

Keep an eye on the cells during the boost charge period; if rapid bubbling is occurring, reduce the charging current immediately.

Continue charging until an electrolyte specific gravity of 1.250 is reached concurrent with an electrolyte temperature of 60°F.

After charging, check the level of electrolyte in all cells and adjust as necessary by adding additional *electrolyte* (not water). The battery is now ready for service.

In the future, if the electrolyte level becomes low, *pure water*—not electrolyte—should be added to the cells.

Installation in the Aircraft

The procedure for installing a new battery in an airplane is the same as that for reinstalling an old one. Start by ensuring that the top of the battery is dry, the cells are properly filled (not overfilled), and the terminal posts are free of corrosion. If the posts are fuzzy, take a wire brush to them.

Before actually connecting any wires to the battery, it is usually a good idea to check the battery's polarity with a voltmeter. Contrary to what you might think, it *is* possible to reverse the polarity of a lead-acid battery (even an old one) by leaving it on a charger with the wires switched around. Check this possibility out before installing the battery in the plane; otherwise, rapid (and costly) damage to solid-state devices may result when you turn on that master switch.

Likewise, be sure—when you lower the battery into its box in the airplane—that the terminal posts face the appropriate lead wires ("+" to red and "-" to black). At the very least, you can expect to blow all the diodes in your alternator if you connect the battery backwards. A good precaution is to keep masking tape over the ends of the lead wires until the battery is finally ready to be hooked up.

When the battery is securely in place and facing the right direction, untape the *positive* wire, slip its end over the positive post of the battery, and tighten the wing nut for that post down onto the wire connector. Then do the same for the negative lead wire. Be sure the wires are tightly secured to the battery. As one Rebat service letter states: "Loose cables will cause hard or no-start conditions and also adds resistance to the electrical system. This resistance prevents the charging system from supplying sufficient current to fully charge the battery, *and can also contribute to RFI (radio interference) as the battery acts as a large capacitor and absorbs stray voltage spikes which may cause RFI.*"

Finally, *after* (not before) the wing nuts are cinched down tight, coat them—and the ends of the lead wires—with petroleum jelly to retard corrosion; then strap the lid back on the battery box, get out your

Recommended Seasonally Adjusted Voltage Regulator Settings		
Ambient Temperature	12 Volt Battery	24 Volt Battery
65°F	14.1 to 14.9	29.2 to 29.8
80°F	13.9 to 14.7	27.8 to 29.4
105°F	13.7 to 14.5	27.4 to 29.0
125°F	13.5 to 14.3	27.0 to 28.6
145°F	13.4 to 14.2	26.8 to 28.4

Part of extending battery life is adjusting the regulator, summer and winter.

aircraft logbook, and make an entry in the log stating the date, tach time, and the nature of the work performed. (For instance: "Battery removed from aircraft this date for servicing i/a/w Beech shop manual instructions page 2-20F. Four tablespoons of water added to each cell. Specific gravity 1.250±.020 for each cell." Or whatever.)

If you've just installed a *new* (and freshly boost-charged) battery in your plane—and you want the battery to hold its charge—you probably should fly the plane for an hour or so, to ensure that the battery is fully activated (and to see that all ammeter indications are normal). By the way, be sure to mention this "test flight" in the *aircraft log* when you're done.

Extending the Battery's Life

The key to attaining extended battery TBRs (time between replacements) is to maintain the proper *amount* and *concentration* of electrolyte in each of the battery's cells at all (or nearly all) times. Failure to do this will result in early battery retirement.

Maintaining the proper amount of electrolyte in each of a battery's cells is extremely important, since damaging sulfate deposits form quickly at the air/metal interface whenever plate material is allowed to become exposed to air. Any time you can look into a cell and see a partially dry plate assembly, chances are some sulfation damage has already occurred. The only "cure" for this is prevention.

The best way to keep the fluid at the optimum level in each cell is not just to check the cells once a month (as is recommended by virtually all airframe manufacturers), but to maintain a logbook record of the amount of water consumed by the various cells per service interval. By starting with frequent servicing intervals (once every two weeks, say) and monitoring water usage accurately to determine each cell's rate of electrolysis, you should be able to determine the *optimum* service interval for *your battery*, in *your plane* —and avoid ever running a cell dry. As the Beech 35 Shop Manual states, "Accurate water consumption data is a valid barometer to use for adjustment of servicing intervals."

Maintaining the electrolyte at its optimum specific gravity (somewhere around 1.250) is just as important to long battery life as keeping the electrolyte level up, since a specific gravity that's too *high* (i.e., too acidic) results in shortened plate life, while a too-*low* specific gravity promotes sulfation (a battery's worst enemy). Keeping the specific gravity up in the winter is no problem. In the summer, however, when the self-discharge rate of a lead-acid battery is considerable (due to the high ambient air temperature), electrolyte specific gravity tends to diminish rapidly unless the plane is flown often or the battery is periodically taken out and put on a charger.

Needless to say, the aircraft voltage regulator plays a critical role in determining battery longevity. If the charging rate is set too low, the battery may never reach a fully-charged state; sulfation is likely to set in during the first relatively long period of inactivity. If the charging output is too high (as is frequently the case), excess amounts of water will be lost through hydrolysis, exposing the plate assemblies to air— and the concentration of sulfuric acid in the electrolyte can reach levels at which plate life is shortened. (Have your voltage regulator adjusted by a competent technician if you suspect that your battery is being overcharged.)

Naturally, getting long life out of a battery also demands that details be looked to properly. The top of the battery, cables, and clamps (and hold-down brackets) must be kept clean. Cables, terminals, and clamps and brackets must be properly adjusted. Loose cables will cause hard or no-start conditions and also add resistance to the electrical system, which, in turn, prevents the charging system from supplying sufficient current to fully charge the battery; it can also encourage RFI, as the battery acts as a large capacitor and absorbs stray voltage spikes which can cause RFI. Avoid these and other abuses, such as allowing the battery to go dead repeatedly and adding hard tap water to the cells.

Like most mechanical creatures, batteries do respond to tender loving care and can be led to grow old gracefully if you keep a sharp eye on their health. This is particularly important when the winds blow hot or cold.

24-Volt Special Considerations

The maintenance requirements of 24-volt batteries are not much different, for the most part, from those of 12-volt aircraft batteries. With few exceptions, everything said thus far in this chapter applies equally to 24-volt batteries. The main difference is that if you own a plane with a 24-volt battery, inadequate attention to your battery's maintenance needs will be far more expensive than it would be if you owned a 12-volter. The 24-volt lead-acid batteries that come in most late-model planes are expensive and unforgiving of neglect.

Where a 12-volt battery consists of *six* cells connected in series, a 24-volt aircraft battery has *twelve* identical cells connected in series. Think of the cells, if you will, as links in a chain. In order for the battery to deliver optimum performance, all cells—all the links in the chain—must be fully functional. If one cell dies, the performance of the entire battery is affected. (A battery with one dead or damaged cell is about as useful as a chain with one broken link.) Simple arithmetic tells you that if a 24-volt battery has twice as many cells as a 12-volt battery, the 24-volter has twice the chance of developing a single bad cell under conditions of inadequate or improper maintenance. This, in a nutshell, is the problem facing the owner of a 24-volt aircraft battery.

A Cessna service letter (SE80-4, dated January 21, 1980) underscores this point by stating: "There is a greater chance for cell damage to occur [in a 24-volt battery, as opposed to a 12-volt battery] if the battery is completely discharged by leaving some electrical system on, such as the master switch or light circuits." Offhand, you might have thought the opposite would be true. You might have thought that a 24-volt battery would be *better* able to withstand the strain of a long, slow discharge (such as occurs when the master switch is accidentally left on) than a smaller 12-volt battery. But not necessarily. In any 24-volt battery, there are inevitably some cells that are weaker than the rest; these cells will discharge deepest and soonest.

The trouble begins when you try to recharge the battery. Getting the lowest cells back up to charge without overcharging the other cells is almost impossible, because you can't recharge the weak cells individually. (The best you can do is charge all twelve cells together, in series.) And yet, if the weakest cells are *not* brought back up to equivalency with the rest of the cells, the service life of the battery will be seriously reduced.

The same factors apply, of course, to *12-volt* batteries that are discharged by leaving the master switch on, but (and this is an important "but") the *difference in charge between the weakest and strongest cells in a six-cell battery is usually much less than the difference in charge between the weakest and strongest cells in a battery with twelve cells.* Generally speaking, the older the battery—and the greater the number of cells in the battery—the more pronounced this difference between weakest and strongest cells is.

Getting one or two (or three) weak cells up to charge after a long drain is perhaps the central problem in 24-volt battery maintenance. Cessna recommends that when a 24-volt battery has been discharged by leaving an electrical circuit on it be [1] removed from the aircraft, and [2] given a constant-current charge at 1.5 amperes until the terminal charge voltage remains constant for three consecutive hours. Alternatively, a constant-voltage type charged can be used. (Again, ideally, the charge rate should be adjusted to 1.5 amps.) When a constant-voltage charger is used, the charging time may go as long as 48 to 72 hours. A long, slow charge is necessary to bring all the cells to a state of parity.

Regardless of the type of charging equipment used, the same precautions that apply to 12-volt battery recharging apply equally to 24-volt battery servicing. That is: care should be taken to see that the battery is placed in a well-ventilated area (no smoking), that the cells are replenished with water as needed, and that cell temperatures never exceed 115°F or 46°C. (If the battery becomes very warm to the touch, the charging rate should be reduced.)

Because a single frozen, dehydrated, or severely sulfated cell can render a 24-volt battery unairworthy, it pays to inspect a 24-volter frequently (once a month, minimum) in order to keep tabs on water consumption, cell gravity, and electrolyte overflow. The latter problem can spell real trouble for the owner of a 24-volt battery for two reasons:

[1] The correction potential with 12-volt batteries (which carry about two quarts of acid) is bad enough; but with 24-volt batteries, which contain over a gallon of electrolyte, even a small amount of overflow from each cell can create a frightening mess. Perhaps it is an exaggeration to say that a 24-volt battery presents twice the corrosion hazard of a 12-volt battery. Then again, perhaps not.

[2] When two puddles of overflowing fluid, from two different cells, touch each other, or when a tiny river of acid connects a cell with a terminal post, a short circuit is created. About an hour later, you have a dead battery.

The new 24-volt batteries, because of their many cells and vent plugs, present interesting possibilities for short circuiting via acid bridges. All you need is for spilled (or overflowing) electrolyte to connect any two cells, and *all the cells between those two cells will short out and undergo rapid self-discharge.* (If you doubt this, dip the ends of a piece of wire in two far-removed cells and watch the cells really start to fizz!)

The same will happen if a stream of spilled electrolyte connects any cell to ground. When the top of the battery gets so damp that an acid bridge is formed *from one battery terminal to the other,* things have definitely gone a bridge too far.

Hence the need to inspect batteries often, and clean up spills quickly.

If moisture is evident on the top of your battery at any time, adhere to the following procedure:

1. Remove the battery from the aircraft, being sure to disconnect the negative (or ground) lead first.

2. Remove the vent plugs from the cells and make a visual check of the electrolyte level. (Observe appropriate safety precautions. Remember, battery fluid is 30 percent sulfuric acid.)

The fluid level must be *above the separators, but below the split ring indicator.* Remove fluid or add pure water as necessary to bring the fluid level to approximately one-eighth of an inch above the tops of the plates.

3. Reinstall the vent plugs tightly, making sure a rubber gasket is present beneath each plug. The use of a silicone grease (Dow Corning DC-7 or equivalent) on the gasket will help ensure a leak-tight seal. Clean away any moisture from the mating surfaces before applying grease.

4. Wash the entire battery (and battery box) with a baking-soda-and-water solution. *Be absolutely sure that no baking soda enters the cells or vent plugs, as permanent damage to the battery will result.* Rinse the battery with water and allow it to dry.

5. Replace the battery in the aircraft, installing the negative (ground) lead last. After (not before) connecting the battery's leads, *apply petroleum jelly to all exposed terminal metal.* This will serve to discourage

short-circuiting due to acid bridging. Also, it will help prevent terminal corrosion due to cell outgassing.

COLD- AND HOT-WEATHER MAINTENANCE

More aircraft batteries die (and have to be replaced) in winter than any other time of year. Maybe you've previously learned this fact, the hard way.

The reasons for cold-weather battery death are simple: the remedies are simpler still. At the heart of the problem is the inescapable fact that lead-acid batteries are miniature *chemical factories*, devices for turning chemical energy into electrical energy (and vice versa). As such, they are subject to the laws of chemistry—one of which is that chemical reaction rates are temperature-dependent. Nearly 100 years ago, the Swedish chemist Arrhenius found that the rate at which a chemical reaction proceeds is influenced in a logarithmic (or exponential) way by temperature.

Reactions not only go faster at higher temperatures, they go *exponentially* faster. The reverse is also true: As temperatures go down, chemical reactions slow down. Not linearly but exponentially.

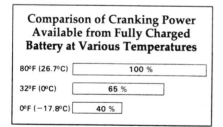

Comparison of Cranking Power Available from Fully Charged Battery at Various Temperatures
80°F (26.7°C) 100 %
32°F (0°C) 65 %
0°F (−17.8°C) 40 %

Figure 1

Comparison of Power Required to Crank Engine With SAE 10W-30 Oil at Various Temperatures
80°F (26.7°C) 100 %
32°F (0°C) 155 %
0°F (−17.8°C) 210 %

Figure 2

Needed: More Cranking Power

The consequences of this for those of us who depend on lead-acid batteries (i.e., chemical reactions) to get our airplane engines going in the morning can be seen in Figure 1. This chart shows the amount of cranking power available from a *fully charged* battery at three different ambient temperatures. Using 80°F as a reference point, we see that when the temperature dips to 32°F, only about two-thirds of normal cranking power is available. At 0°F, the battery will crank only 40 percent as hard as it would at 80°F. (Perhaps, instead of pre-heating our engines on cold days, we ought to be thinking about pre-heating our batteries. More about that below.)

So much for power *available*. Now let's look at the power *required* to crank an engine at various ambient temperatures. In Figure 2, we see clearly that as the temperature drops, and as crankcase oil thickens, cranking friction increases very rapidly, even when a lightweight oil is used. (If you've got SAE 40- or, heaven forbid, SAE 50-weight oil in your sump, your engine may require *four or five times* as much cranking power on a 0°F day as on a warm day.)

Compare Figure 1 with Figure 2 and you can see that as the temperature goes down, cranking requirements go up very rapidly while *power available* takes a nosedive (an exponential nosedive). It's easy to get behind the power curve, so to speak, with a *fully charged* battery—let alone a partially charged one. To see how a partially charged battery fares with respect to all of this, look at Figure 3. Here all of the data from Figure 1 is reprinted along with corresponding data for a half-charged—and nearly discharged—battery. Note that at 32°F, a half-charged battery can put out barely one third of the cranking power of a fully charged 80° battery. At 0°F, a half-charged unit gives only 21 percent of the power produced by a fully charged battery at 80°F. (That's if it doesn't freeze and burst.) Things get rough with a nearly discharged battery.

Comparison Showing How States Of Charge Affect Cranking Power At Various Temperatures

(Showing Percentages Compared to Capacity in the Fully Charged State at 80°F [2.67°C] equal to 100%)

80°F (26.7°C)		
100 %		FULL CHARGE
46 %	1.190—HALF CHARGE	
25 %	1.155—NEARLY DISCHARGED	

32°F (0°C)		
65 %	1.265—FULL CHARGE	
32 %	1.190—HALF CHARGE	
16 %	1.155—NEARLY DISCHARGED	

0°F (−17.8°C)		
40 %	1.265—FULL CHARGE	
21 %	1.190—HALF CHARGE	
9 %	1.155—NEARLY DISCHARGED	

(IN DANGER OF DAMAGE BY FREEZING)

Figure 3

Freezing Point Depression

Still another given of chemistry comes into play with lead-acid batteries in winter-

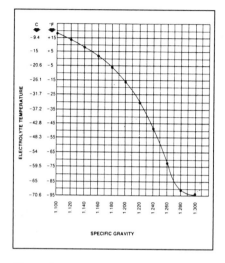

Figure 4

time, the "freezing point depression" law, which says, simply, that as an aqueous solution (battery electrolyte) accumulates more and more solute (sulfuric acid), the solution's freezing point goes down. This law, as it pertains to battery acid, is graphically depicted in Figure 4. What we see here is that a full charged battery with an electrolyte specific gravity (or density relative to pure water) of 1.280 can withstand exposure to temperatures as low as *minus 90°F* without freezing. By contrast, the electrolyte in a nearly discharged battery (gravity: 1.100) will freeze solid at or below about +17°F. Because battery acid is mostly water (90 percent water, in the case of a poorly charged battery), and because water expands when it freezes, the usual result of a battery freezing is bursting of the battery. At that point, you've got a broken battery . . . *and* (if the temperature rises back above the freezing point) battery acid everywhere.

The point of all this would seem to be that if you want your battery to perform adequately (and not freeze up) in cold weather, you should fly often enough so that the battery is kept at a high charge level. Unfortunately, though, it's not that simple. The problems of high-power demands, low-power output, low temperatures, and low state of charge are self-compounding. It so happens (and this is something most pilots do not fully appreciate) that at low temperatures, lead-acid batteries *simply will not accept a charge* as easily as they will at higher temperatures. At 80°F, a half-charged battery will accept approximately 25 to 30 amperes of charging current at 14.4 volts. At 0°F, the same battery will accept *only 2 amperes* under the same charging conditions.

The ramifications of this are startling. On the first good, cold day of winter, the process of starting your engine, turning on your radios, and holding on the taxiway for an IFR clearance while the engine idles (i.e., while the generator is turning over too slowly to charge the battery) may drain your battery to the 50 percent charged state. At your assigned cruising altitude, the outside air temperature may be 0°F (or even lower), and if you cruise for two or three hours, your battery (especially if it is back in the tailcone) will probably be refrigerated to that temperature—in which case it will not be capable of accepting more than an ampere or two of charge current. A trickle charge of one to two amps for two to three hours is not enough to cause a noticeable change in the gravity of a half-charged battery's fluid. Thus, on your *next* flight, you'll be starting out with a half-charged battery. On the flight after that—if low temperatures continue to prevail—you may be the proud owner of a dead, or frozen, battery.

Cold-Weather Comforts

The point is, it's going to take more than regular, frequent flights in your plane to keep the battery up to charge in cold weather. In particular, it's going to take occasional (perhaps monthly, perhaps bimonthly) recharging of the battery *outside the plane*. (Increasing the voltage regulator setting will help keep your battery charged in the plane; however, the voltage regulator's output should never be adjusted more than a small amount, and a small adjustment isn't going to solve the cold-weather charging problem completely. The only answer is to put the battery on a charger from time to time.)

Fortunately, it is very easy to remove the battery from most airplanes, which means that you can lift the battery out of its box and take it home with you after every flight, or after every other flight, in cold weather. Once home, you can put the battery on a small charger, adhering to the charge-rate recommendations given on the side of the battery, and leaving the battery on the charger until the gravity comes up (or until the battery gets warm to the touch, whichever comes first). When it comes time to fly, you can take the battery with you to the airport, install it during your walkaround inspection (installation takes about 30 seconds when you're familiar with the routine) and crank your engine over without fear of killing your battery. (The battery will not only be fully charged from having sat on the charger at home, but it will also be nice and warm and thus capable of delivering warm-day cranking performance.)

Taking the battery home with you during cold spells means investing a relatively few dollars in a good hydrometer (for making charge measurements) and in a 12-volt charger.

Incidentally, there is a *good* side to cold-weather battery mainte-

Leave a battery in the cold at a low charge state, and it will freeze and burst.

nance. Thanks to the temperature/reaction-rate relationship discussed earlier, batteries undergo a much slower rate of self-discharge at low temperatures than they do at high temperatures, which means that once your battery is fully charged, it will stay that way for a long time in the winter between uses. (You can let a fully charged battery sit idle for a month at 32°F without seeing a noticeable change in electrolyte gravity.)

Also, at low temperatures, the rate of lead sulfate formation on a battery's plates is greatly retarded. Thus, again, you can neglect a fully charged—or even a half-charged—battery for weeks without seeing noticeable changes in its chemistry.

Heated Reactions

If your battery made it through the winter, you may be tempted to think that the hardest part of the year (from the battery's viewpoint) is over. No more charge-depleting cold starts; no more worry about cells freezing and bursting in sub-zero weather. No more worry about whether the voltage regulator's charge setting is high enough to keep the battery up. (Ice-cold batteries won't charge as easily as warm batteries, at a given voltage.)

But hot weather imposes its own unique demands. Believe it or not, inactivity takes a much heavier toll on a battery in summer than in winter (assuming that it begins each season with a full charge). Self-discharge occurs through diffusion and chemical reaction at the plates. These processes are, of course, temperature-dependent; and reactions not only go faster at high temperature, they go *exponentially* faster. Leave your battery standing for 10 days at an OAT of 30°F, and it will still have about 98 percent of its original charge when you check it again. But leave your battery standing at an OAT of 100°F, and it will have lost 25 percent of its charge in only 10 days. (Every 10 days thereafter, it will lose 25 percent of the residual charge.)

As a result of the temperature effect—which results not only in faster self-discharge, but in more vigorous recharging when in use—a wet-cell battery tends to outgas liberally in warmer weather, which of course is a pleasant way of saying that your battery box and cable ends are going to look like a mess if you don't clean them up every few weeks. The problem with outgassing is not only one of corrosion (and sheer unsightly wetness), but potential coating of the top of the battery with acid. What happens when a thin, sticky layer of (highly conductive) acid forms on top of the battery, in turn, is that cell bridging can occur. When two adjacent cells are acid-bridged, the resulting short causes a deep-discharge that can never be corrected. Those two cells can never be brought back up to par; the plates are shot. You just bought yourself a battery.

Owners of fuel-injected planes (with Lycoming IO-360 engines, particularly) tend to have shorter battery life than their carbureted kin, quite often, due to the extra cranking that accompanies hot starts in summer. You'd think cold-cranking would impose a greater burden on batteries than extended cranking in warm-OAT conditions, but t'ain't necessarily so. Extreme cold effectively prohibits a battery from delivering amperage at maximal rate—in essence, the cold provides a built-in flow-limiter, a safety valve of sorts. In hot weather, by contrast, the battery (due to the laws of Arrhenius) over-exerts itself very quickly and effectively. Extended cranking

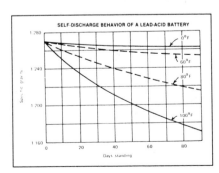

SELF-DISCHARGE BEHAVIOR OF A LEAD-ACID BATTERY

of a vapor-locked engine can cause the battery's plates to heat up to the point that they warp and spall. (It doesn't do your starter motor much good, either.) Battery temperatures soar in a hot-weather "hung start," particularly when the battery is firewall-mounted (and thus subject to heat soakback from the engine). Then, after the engine finally comes to life, the alternator and voltage regulator go to work, and the deep-discharged battery starts fizzing like a flooded Alka-Seltzer factory. See what you're up against?

So don't neglect your battery in warm weather. If you haven't already done so, buy a good hydrometer ("good" meaning small—small enough to work with tiny quantities of electrolyte, which is all you'll ever aspirate from an airplane battery—but with a numerical scale rather than just a color scale, or, heaven forbid, a bunch of floating pith balls), either at the local auto parts store or through one of the big pilot's mail order houses.

Also invest in a metal brush with which to clean terminal connections. (Get this locally, at your hardware or department store.) Stash some paper towels and baking soda in the plane, for use in cleaning up acid spills on and around the battery; and coat terminal lugs with Vaseline between look-sees. (It'll stave off corrosion.)

Also remember to keep fresh water handy (for emergencies), and observe proper safety precautions. Battery acid eats through aluminum; it will eat through clothing, skin, and eyes too.

When disconnecting cables, remember to remove the ground (negative) connection *first*, and reconnect it *last*. And be sure to keep the connections tight (use lockwashers).

As we have seen, while most of the work pertaining to your airplane's "nervous system" lies in the domain of licensed technicians, you need not be isolated from the maintenance loop. There is much that you can do to affirm the integrity and comfortability of the panel by which you fly. You can also be involved in the protection of your electrical resources, if only to know how they work and how they can fail. For the conscientious IFR pilot, certainly, that is essential, but even VFR airmen who want to use their aircraft to the fullest do well to become educated along these lines. The rewards for doing so can multiply dramatically. Seize them and enjoy.

APPENDICES

Appendix A

GYRO INSTRUMENT TROUBLESHOOTING

The information presented below has been assembled from many different sources and is general in nature. For more detailed information on the design, operation, and maintenance of vacuum systems (and components), refer to Chapter 2, as well as appropriate maintenance manuals for the individual instruments.

Gyro Horizon

SYMPTOM	POSSIBLE CAUSES	REMEDY
Horizon bar fails to respond.	Central and/or instrument air filter dirty.	Check filter at rear of instrument; clean or replace as needed. Also check central air filter, if one is used.
	Suction relief valve improperly adjusted.	Readjust per aircraft manual specs.
	Faulty suction gauge.	Substitute a known-good gauge and check gyro operation. replace old gauge, if necessary.
	Vacuum pump (or venturi) failure.	Replace unit.

SYMPTOM	POSSIBLE CAUSES	REMEDY
	Vacuum line kinked or leaking.	Check all connections for tightness; repair or replace damaged lines.
Horizon bar does not settle.	Defective mechanism.	Substitute a known-good gyro horizon to confirm. Replace instrument if necessary.
	Insufficient vacuum.	Adjust suction relief valve.
	Excessive vibration.	Inspect panel shock mounts. Check cylinder compression, condition of spark plugs.
Horizon bar oscillates or vibrates.	Central or instrument filter dirty.	Check air filter at rear of instrument and replace if necessary. Check main vacuum air filter if instrument filter is clean.
	Suction relief valve improperly adjusted.	Adjust or replace valve as needed.
	Faulty suction gauge.	Substitute a known-good gauge and check gyro response. Replace gauge if necessary.

SYMPTOM	POSSIBLE CAUSES	REMEDY
	Defective mechanism.	Substitute a known-good gyro and check its operation.
	Excessive vibration.	Check panel shock mounts; also check engine condition.
Excessive drift in either direction.	Low vacuum.	Check suction relief valve for proper setting.
	Vacuum line kinked or leaking.	Check security of all line connections. Replace damaged lines.
	Vacuum pump (or venturi) failure.	Check unit and replace, if necessary.
	Faulty suction gauge.	Substitute a known-good gauge and check gyro operation; replace old gauge if need be.
Hand does not indicate proper turn.	Hand out of calibration.	Have instrument calibrated.
	Defective mechanism.	Replace instrument
Hand vibrates.	Damping screw not set properly.	Have screw adjusted.

SYMPTOM	POSSIBLE CAUSES	REMEDY
	Excessive panel vibration.	Check panel for condition. Check engine compression, ignition system integrity.
	Defective mechanism.	Replace instrument.
Pointer fails to respond.	Inlet cap or screen is clogged.	Clean or replace as necessary.
	Oil is too thick (cold temperatures).	Allow oil to warm up.
Incorrect sensitivity.	Vacuum too low or too high (check suction gauge indications).	Adjust suction relief valve; check all lines, connections; replace dirty filters.
	Inlet cap or screen is clogged.	Clean or replace as necessary.
	Sensitivity spring defective.	Replace instrument.

Turn & Bank (Vacuum Operated)

SYMPTOM	POSSIBLE CAUSES	REMEDY
Instrument gives fluctuating indications.	Leak in line or instrument.	Check all lines for integrity. Repair or replace instrument.

SYMPTOM	POSSIBLE CAUSES	REMEDY
	Vacuum supply fluctuating or improperly adjusted.	Check system for constant, correct vacuum. Check panel shock mounts, vacuum filters, vacuum pump.
	Damaged gyro.	Repair or replace instrument.
Gyro fails to start.	Clogged filter.	Check instrument filter, system filter.
	Low vacuum.	Adjust suction relief valve; check vacuum pump, system plumbing for integrity.
	Oil is too thick (low temperatures).	Allow time for oil to warm up.

Appendix B

PITOT-STATIC INSTRUMENT TROUBLESHOOTING

Note: The following information is presented for educational purposes only. FAR Part 43, Appendix A, allows pilots to replace "any hose connection except hydraulic connections"; however, some of the procedures mentioned below are best accomplished by professional maintenance personnel. Consult FAR Part 43 before undertaking any of the following procedures.

Altimeter

SYMPTOM	POSSIBLE CAUSES	REMEDY
Incorrect indications.	Shift in mechanism.	Have instrument recalibrated.
	Leaking diaphragm.	Replace instrument.
	Hands not set accurately.	Reset hands.
Instrument fails to operate.	Static line plugged.	Open alternate static source. If instrument still fails to function, blockage is in line from airspeed indicator to altimeter. If alternate static source restores

SYMPTOM	POSSIBLE CAUSES	REMEDY
		function, obstruction is in main static source line. blow line clear.
	Defective mechanism.	Replace instrument.
Pointer oscillates.	Static irregular.	Check lines for obstruction or leaks. Blow out lines and/or re-tighten connections as necessary.
	Leak in altimeter case.	Repair or replace instrument.
	Leak in static connections to other instruments.	Check plumbing from altimeter to other instruments. Blow out lines, tighten connections.

Airspeed Indicator

SYMPTOM	POSSIBLE CAUSES	REMEDY
Instrument fails to operate.	Pitot line clogged.	Check pitot tube; remove and clean if necessary. (Cover between flights to avoid contamination.) Blow out pitot

SYMPTOM	POSSIBLE CAUSES	REMEDY
		line, retighten connections.
	Pitot line broken or improperly connected.	Replace line or tighten connections.
	Damaged instrument.	Replace.
Pointer vibrates.	Excessive panel vibration.	Check panel mounts.
	Tubing vibration.	Check tubing clamps.
Pointer wavers.	Damaged instrument (ruptured diaphragm, defective mechanism, etc.)	Replace unit.
	Leak in other instruments.	Inspect/repair static lines connecting ASI, altimeter, and ROC indicator.
	Leak in main pitot or static line.	Tighten connections or replace lines as necessary.

Rate of Climb Indicator

SYMPTOM	POSSIBLE CAUSES	REMEDY
Does not indicate zero in level flight.	Aging diaphragm.	Return pointer to zero with reset knob. Tap instrument lightly.

SYMPTOM	POSSIBLE CAUSES	REMEDY
Instrument inoperative.	Clogged static line. (Condensation, insects, etc.)	If alternate static source returns function, blockage is between ROC and other instruments. Otherwise, blow out all lines.
	Static line leak(s).	Repair leaks.
	Defective instrument.	Replace unit.
Pointer oscillates.	Clogged static line.	Blow out line.
	Leak in static line.	Repair line
	Leaky instrument case.	Repair/replace unit.
Pointer vibrates.	See above (Airspeed Indicator section).	

Appendix C

MANIFOLD PRESSURE GAUGE TROUBLESHOOTING

Note: The following information is presented for educational purposes only. Part 43 of the Federal Aviation Regulations defines who may and may not perform various classes of maintenance on normal category U.S. aircraft. The reader is advised to consult FAR Part 43 before undertaking any of the procedures mentioned in these charts.

SYMPTOM	POSSIBLE CAUSES	REMEDY
High M.P. at idle.	Air leak in induction system.	Have system checked and—if necessary—repaired.
	Hydraulic lifters are bleeding down too fast.	Lifters should be replaced.
	Incorrect hydraulic lifters installed.	Check part numbers and (if needed) install correct lifters.
	Improperly adjusted carburetor or fuel injector.	Have mechanic check and adjust idle mixture.
M.P. gauge operates sluggishly.	Foreign matter in pressure line.	Have mechanic check line and

SYMPTOM	POSSIBLE CAUSES	REMEDY
		blow out foreign matter.
	Leak in pressure line.	Have line inspected. See that all connections are properly tightened; if that doesn't solve the problem (or if line is obviously damaged), replace line.
	Gauge mechanism is dirty.	Remove/replace gauge.
Gauge reads 29" to 30" at all times.	Broken pressure line.	Replace line.
	Faulty mechanism.	Replace instrument.
Excessive needle vibration.	Tight rocker pivot bearings.	Replace instrument.
	Excessive panel vibration.	Inspect and replace panel shock mounts as necessary.
Gauge operates in erratic fashion.	Leak in pressure line.	Test line and connections. Repair/replace line. Tighten all connections as needed.
	Faulty mechanism.	Replace instrument.

SYMPTOM	POSSIBLE CAUSES	REMEDY
Excessive gauge error with engine stopped.	Condensate or fuel in line.	Have line blown out.
	Leak in pressure line.	(see above)
	Leak in vacuum bellows.	Replace instrument.
	Loose pointer (or pointer has shifted).	Replace instrument.

Appendix D

BATTERY TROUBLESHOOTING

Note: Some of these procedures call for use of continuity testing equipment. There are three main types of continuity testers: One is the portable "dry cell" type tester having a buzzer or a 3-volt lamp to indicate the completed circuit; this device is used to test continuity with the main circuit *off*. Another tester is the "hot light" (an ordinary 12-volt bulb with one wire soldered to each terminal), which is used to test circuits with the main circuit *on.* A third type of tester (also used when the main circuit in *on*) is the precision voltmeter.

SYMPTOM	POSSIBLE CAUSES	REMEDY
Dead battery.	Standing too long. "Too long" can be as little as one week of inactivity.	Remove/recharge battery. Make note of specific gravity of electrolyte before and after charging. At 70°F, a gravity reading of 1.256 indicates a 75% charge.
	Master switch and/ or equipment accidentally left on.	Recharge battery.
	Impure electrolyte.	Replace battery.
	Short to ground in wiring.	Check wiring with continuity testing equipment.

SYMPTOM	POSSIBLE CAUSES	REMEDY
	Broken cell partitions.	Replace battery.
	Battery not being charged at the proper rate by alterrnator/ generator.	First consider whether you're using so much electrical equipment on every flight that your battery rarely has a chance to recharge. (If so, turn off some equipment.) If this is not the problem, ask your mechanic to check the voltage regulator setting and adjust it if necessary.
	Battery is worn out (in which case it won't recharge no matter what you do).	Replace battery.
Short battery life.	Insufficient electrolyte.	Replace electrolyte on a regular basis by adding *distilled water* to the cells.
	Impure electrolyte.	Replace battery.
	Repeated heavy discharge.	Lessen electrical load. (I.e., turn off some equipment,

SYMPTOM	POSSIBLE CAUSES	REMEDY
		reduce starter use on ground.)
	Sulfation due to disuse.	Fly the plane ! You may be able to save the life of a sulfated battery by trickle-charging it for 50 to 100 hours at half the recommended charge rate. Otherwise, you'll need a new battery.
Cracked cells.	Hold-down bracket loose.	Install new battery, secure firmly.
	Battery was allowed to freeze.	Keep new battery charged. (Replace existing battery.) A 75%-charged battery is unfreezable down to minus 62°F. NOTE: Always charge battery for one half hour minimum following addition of water in freezing weather.
Excessive water consumption in all cells.	Charging rate too high (Compound on top of battery may be melted; check this.)	Have charging rate adjusted.

SYMPTOM	POSSIBLE CAUSES	REMEDY
Excessive water consumption in one cell only.	Cracked cell.	Replace battery.
Corrosion inside container.	Charging rate too high.	Have charging rate adjusted.
	Spillage from overfilling cells.	Flush container with baking soda solution.
	Leaking or clogged vent lines.	Clean out lines.
Electrolyte runs out of vent plugs.	Too much water added to battery.	Drain off some electrolyte; maintain at proper level.

INDEX

Index

Aerosafe, Inc. 46
Air Capital Instruments 9
Air-oil separator
    (also see Vacuum system maintenance) 32
    FAA rule on cleaning 38
    maintenance 32, 37
    problems 37
    reinstallation 38
    reinstallation, log entry 38
    removal 38
Airborne
    Division of Parker Hannifin 49
    vacuum pumps .... 39 ff.
Aircraft Components Inc. 84
Aircraft Instrument and Development Inc. 83
Aircraft Owners and Pilots Association (AOPA) 18
Aircraft Spruce and Specialty Co. 22
Airpath Instrument Co. 12
Alcor .... 78 ff.
Alternator problems
    broken field winding 116
    diode failure 116
    non-alternator causes 115
    open "Y" 117
    open field circuit .... 116 ff.
    shorted field winding 116
    shorted stator winding 117
Alternator servicing
    alternator servicing 115-123
    alternative strategies 115
    belts and pulleys checks 118
    peak-to-peak testing 119-122
    peak-to-peak voltmeter .... 119 ff.
    repair options 123
    safety cautions 118
    Support Systems Analyzer .... 121 ff.
    troubleshooting 116-123

Alternator servicing, continued
   troubleshooting diode failure ....118 ff.
   troubleshooting with fingernail test 117
   troubleshooting with hot-light ....117 ff.
   troubleshooting with oscilloscope ....119 ff.
AOPA *Handbook for Pilots* 18
Arrhenius, Swedish chemist (19th century) 161
Ashby, Dennis 18
Avionics
   airframe and installation effects 95
   industry problems 89
   obsolescence and quality control 89
   radio interference (RFI) from batteries ....156 ff.
   threats to longevity ....89 ff.
   water and heat effects 90
Avionics maintenance
   avionics maintenance 90-97
   cleaning contacts 94
   frequency-selector wafer switches 94
   navcom frequency loss 94
   navcom reinstallation 94
   navcom removal 93
   Nuvistor tubes 93
   protection from heat, avoiding overuse 91
   protection from heat, cooling devices 91
   protection from heat, sunscreen 90
   protection from moisture 90
   transponder antenna problems 96
   troubleshooting, vital questions 95
   TSO requirements, heat 91
   tube checking 93
   tube degradation 92
   tube replacement, FAA policy 94
Batteries
   (also see Generator maintenance) 143
   (also see Voltage regulators) 143
   24-volt batteries 159
   24-volt, additional vulnerability ....159 ff.
   24-volt, greater corrosion hazard 160
   24-volt, short circuit hazards...161

Batteries, continued
    causes of radio interference (RFI) .... 156 ff.
    cold weather, effects of cranking 162
    cold weather, self-discharge benefit 164
    cold-weather drain 162
    FAA AC 43.13-1A on battery life 149
    FAA requirements 154
    heavy cranking effects 150
    hot weather, corrosion and damage 167
    hot weather, self-discharge problems 165
    master switch left on 150
    sulfation causes and effects 152
    sulfation remedy 152
Battery maintenance
    24-volt battery, moisture remedy 161
    24-volt battery, recharging 160
    30-day check .... 144 ff.
    activating dry-charged batteries 155
    adding water 149
    basic procedures 143-150
    battery hydrometer .... 145 ff.
    battery life extension .... 157 ff.
    charge level check 149
    charge level measurement .... 145 ff.
    chargers 151
    charging 150-152
    cold weather.. 162 ff.
    cold weather, removal and recharging 165
    corrosion inspection and removal 149
    electrolyte level maintenance 157
    electrolyte specific gravity check 148
    electrolyte specific gravity maintenance 157
    electrolyte specific gravity, temperature effects.......................... 149
    hot weather .... 166 ff.
    hot weather, safety caution 168
    hot weather, use of battery hydrometer 168
    inspection 147
    inspection, Exide AC-78M 148
    inspection, Willard W-78M 148
    installation 156

Batteries, continued
  installation cautions 156
  lead-acid batteries, aircraft vs. automobiles 144
  logbook entry 157
  logging battery water consumption 157
  polarity reversal dangers 156
  purchasing options, makes 153
  Rebat R-35 charging instructions 151
  removal from aircraft 146
  replacement .... 153 ff.
  replacement, when to buy 154
  safety caution 145, 147, 152
  servicing intervals .... 143 ff.
  servicing intervals, Beech recommendations 144
  voltage regulator monitoring and adjustment 157
Beech Aircraft
  Bonanza 16
  C35 Bonanza 19
  Duchess 16
  Model 35 *Shop Manual* 144
  Sierra 16
  Sundowner 16
  panel designs 16
  panel labeling 24
Candle Aviation Supply 14
Carburetor temperature gauge
  (also see Cylinder head temperature gauge) 83
  power supply check 5
Century Instrument Corp. 9
Cessna Aircraft
  altimeter leakage recommendation 54
  Cessna aircraft 98
  Cessna180 16
  Cessna 210 series 44
  Cessna 310 52
  Cessna P210 49
  Skylane 15
  Skylane .... 97 ff.
  battery locations 146
  false panel construction 7

Cessna Aircraft, continued
  panel designs 16
  panel labeling 24
  suction tubing...32
  24-volt battery recharging recommendations 160
Cylinder Head Temperatures (CHT)
  checking power supply...5
  CHT/carb temp gauge ....81 ff.
  CHT/carb temp gauge installation ....83 ff.
  CHT/carb temp gauge installation, tools and materials ....83 ff.
  CHT/carb temp gauge panel mounting 84
  logging CHT/carb temp gauge installation 86
  Richter B-5 resistance probe 83
Cleansers
  Bon-Ami 149
  Varsol...126
Cockpit speaker
  depth 98
  impedance matching 98
  magnet's effect on compass...98
  reinstallation 98
  removal 97
  replacement selection 98
  replacement 97-99
Contacts
  contacts 106-113
  burnishing tool 111
  checking with ohmmeter 108
  cleaning through arcing and friction 111
  cleaning toggle switches 112
  cleaning wafer switches 113
  cleaning with alcohol 108
  cleaning with bond paper...110
  cleaning, voltage regulator 140
  color-TV tuner cleaner 110
  color-TV tuner cleaner, on wafer switches 113
  contact melt...111
  corrosion ....109 ff.
  design and operation..107
  indigenous problems..106

Contacts, continued
protecting metal while cleaning 111
PTT switches 107
relay switches 108
toggle switches 107
Continental engines
oil circulation 60
oil pressure pickoff locations 60
Corrosion
batteries, inspection and removal 149
chemical action 109
contacts 109
Cylinder head temperature
fuel gauge loss 56
indications after hard start 56
Delco-Remy 127
Douglas DC-4 34
Edo (Sigma-Tec) vacuum pumps .... 39 ff.
Exhaust Gas Temperature (EGT)
all-cylinder displays, analog 77-79
all-cylinder displays, digital 79-81
checking power supply 5
combined with CHT 76, 79
digital vs. analog 75
effect of carburetor heat 56
GEM Model 602 Graphic Engine Monitor 79
leanest and hottest cylinder 70
misconceptions .... 70 ff.
multi-probe advantages 70
non-amplified vs. amplified gauge 57
numeric presentation disadvantages 75
recently developed capabilities 71
scanner difficulties 76
scanners 76
switchable EGT advantages and disadvantages 72
trend monitoring advantages 74
upgrading .... 71 ff.
value of numerical indications 70
widened spread indications 58
zeroing out, pros and cons 78

Electro-Mech 46
Electronics International 72
Emergency Locator Transmitter (ELT)
   ELT 103
   antenna 106
   disassembly 103
   function check 105
   legal flight operations without 103
   logging replacement 106
   Narco ELT-10 ....104 ff.
   reassembly and installation 104
   Sharc 7 or Merl 104
Engine instruments
   (also see Cylinder Head Temperature).......................70
   (also see Exhaust gas temperature) 71
   (also see Manifold pressure gauge).............................55
   (also see Oil pressure indicator) 55
   (also see Tachometer) 55
   fuel flow gauge...57
   fuel flow gauge breakage 59
   fuel gauge loss and CHT 57
   manifold pressure gauge indications 57
   oil gauges required for flight 56
Ergonomics, instrument panels..16
Exide AC-78M battery (affected by AD 79-07-02) 148
FAA Advisory Circular AC 43.13-1A (battery life) 149
FAA Form 337 ....19, 21, 86
FAA maintenance policies
   air filter maintenance 49
   air-oil separator servicing 38
   avionics tubes 94
   batteries 154
   generator belt replacement.......................................125
   instrument panel refashioning....................................18
   logging tachometer maintenance 69
   requirement for instrument markings 9
   static system check 54
   static system, repetition of check 53
   tachometer repair...66
   vacuum system valve screen cleaning........................37

Federal Aviation Regulations
FAR 21 49
FAR 43 ....37, 38
FAR 43.13 154
FAR 43.3(d) 15
FAR 65.81 12
FAR 91.171 ....53, 54
FAR 91.33 ....10, 57
FAR 91.52 103
Frey, Ray 17
G.R. Lowe 103
Generator (DC) maintenance
A&P signoff 125
armature servicing..133
armature servicing caution....................................133
belt inspection, deflection method 125
belt inspection, torque method 124
belt replacement..125
belt retightening..125
belt tension gauge 124
belt tension inspection 124-125
belt tension, Lycoming recommendations 125
brush installation 126
brushes and brush tension inspection ....126 ff.
commutator inspection 126
Delco 127
Delco-Remy generator design and operation..............128
Delco-Remy generator regular maintenance 128
external connections and wiring inspection 125
field coil servicing..132
field coil servicing caution......................................133
generator mounting inspection 125
inspection intervals 123
Piper Aircraft recommendations ....123 ff.
repolarization 134
troubleshooting (Delco-Remy)............................128-135
troubleshooting, battery charge................................129
troubleshooting, excessive output............................132
troubleshooting, no output 132
troubleshooting, noisy generator 132

Generator maintenance, continued
    troubleshooting, unsteady or low output 132
    troubleshooting, use of growler ....131 ff.
    troubleshooting, use of test lamp 130
    troubleshooting, use of test points 130
    troubleshooting, voltage regulator...129
    voltage regulator 129
Gyro instrument maintenance
    removal and reinstallation 49
    filter inspection and replacement 49
    installation, aircraft leveling 50
ICT Instrument Inc. 9
Insight Instrument Corp. 72
Instrument panel protection
    from fluid leaks 10
    from heat 9
Instrument panel refashioning
    Beech aircraft panel design 16
    C35 Bonanza 19
    Cessna aircraft panel design 16
    countersinking gauges in Plexiglas 25
    decals 25
    detailing ....24 ff.
    ergonomic considerations 16
    FAA Form 337 19
    FAA requirements ....18 ff.
    label application ....25 ff.
    labeling, manufacturers' methods..25
    Mooney Aircraft..18
    painting 24
    panel refashioning ....15 ff.
    Piper Comanche...17
    Presstype ....26 ff.
    static system check 21
Instrument panel renovation
    basic tools...4
    false panels in Cessna aircraft 7
    instrument attach screws and nuts 8
    instrument removal...6-8
    instrument suppliers 9

Instrument panel renovation, continued
   reassembly ....8 ff.
   regulations regarding range markings 9
   seat removal 4
Instrument panel troubleshooting
   troubleshooting 5-8
   hydraulic pump 6
   hydraulic pump installations 5
   power sources ....5 ff.
   vacuum source 5-8
   VSI resetting 9
J. C. Whitney 151
J.P. Instruments..76
Kelly Instruments 9
King radios 109
KS Avionics ....72, 77 ff.
Logbook entries
   air-oil separator 38
   battery servicing 157
   battery water consumption 157
   CHT/carb temp gauge installation 86
   ELT replacement 106
   magnetic compass maintenance 15
   static system check 54
   tachometer maintenance..66, 69
Lycoming engines
   approved for CHT/carb temp gauges..................................84
   generator/alternator belt tension recommendations 124
   on CHT and oil temperature readings................................81
   oil circulation 60
Magnetic compass
   card error 10
   card oscillation 10
   compass swinging 12
   construction and operation 13
   diaphragm replacement...13
   diaphragm replacement, FAA rules 15
   federal maintenance restrictions 12
   federal requirement 10
   fluid replenishment 12

Magnetic compass, continued
  logbook entry 15
  maintenance 11-15
  MIL-C5020A compass fluid 14
Manifold pressure gauge
  indications 57
  manifold vs. deck pressure 59
Marque club 18
Merl Inc. 104
Midwest Aircraft Instruments 9
Miller Air Sports 18
Mooney Aircraft
  M20J (201) 61
  panel designs 18
  Super 21 18
Oil pressure indicator
  Bourdon tube breakage 56
  indicator, general 59-63
  hydraulic vs. electric 61
  interpreting indications 61
  maintenance precautions 62
  oil circulation systems 60
  oil pressure and power settings 61
  oil pressure and prop governors 62
  oil pressure and viscosity 61
  pressure pickoff locations 60
  pressure ticks 62
  required for flight 56
  troubleshooting low pressure .... 61 ff.
Oils and additives
  Aeroshell Multigrade 62
  Marvel Mystery Oil 62
  Microlon 62
  Phillips X/C 62
Painting, instrument panel 24
Pamco Industries 42, 43
Parker Hannifin, Airborne Division 49
Piper Aircraft
  Comanche .... 17, 22, 25 ff., 82
  battery locations 146

Piper Aircraft, continued
    generator maintenance recommendations .... 123 ff.
    instruments' heat vulnerability 10
    Lance 79
    panel labeling 25
    Seminole .... 78 ff.
Pitot-static system
    (also see Static system) 31
    alternate static source 52
    avoiding pressure spikes 54
    blocked-tube indications 52
    causes of blockage 51
    check during panel refashioning 21
    handling anomalous indications 49
    maintenance 49-54
    pitot heat 54
    pitot tube blockage prevention 52
    pitot tube covers 52
    protection from water 52
Quam-Nichols Co. 99
Radio Systems Technology 108
Rockwell Aero Commander, panel labeling 25
Sealant, Dow Corning DC-7 161
Sherman, Gene 154
Sky Sales 25
Solvents
    Prep-Sol 26, 28
    Stoddard 38
    Varsol 38, 41
Static system
    (also see Pitot-static system) 31
    blockage and alternate static source .... 52 ff.
    blockage and instrument errors .... 52 ff.
    blockage and pilot error .... 52 ff.
Static system check
    after panel refashioning 21
    altimeter leakage 54
    avoiding suction spikes 54
    Baumanometer use 54
    FAA requirement 54

Static system check, continued
    FAA requirement to repeat 53
    logging 54
    system check 53-54
    troubleshooting 54
Stockhill, Michael L. ....24 ff., 66
Strobe system
    caution against reversing polarity 101
    caution in checking power supply 101
    caution in powering up 100
    design 99
    effects of inactivity 99
    electrolytic capacitor degradation 99
Strobe system troubleshooting
    flash tube checks 102
    flash tube problems ....102 ff.
    harness continuity checks 101
    power supply checks 100
    problem location 100
    safety cautions 101
    troubleshooting 99-103
Suppliers
    Aerosafe Inc. 46
    Air Capital Instruments 9
    Aircraft Components Inc. 84
    Aircraft Instrument and Development Inc.
    (R..C. Allen Instrument Division) 83
    Aircraft Spruce and Specialty Co. 22, 26
    Airpath Instrument Co. 12
    Alcor ....78 ff.
    Ashby, Dennis 18
    Candle Aviation Supply 14
    Century Instrument Corp. 9
    Delco-Remy 127
    Electro-Mech 46
    Electronics International 72
    Frey, Ray 17
    ICT Instrument Inc. 9
    Insight Instrument Corp. 72
    J. C. Whitney 151

Suppliers, continued
    J.P. Instruments 76
    Kelly Instruments, Inc. 9
    KS Avionics ....72, 77 ff.
    Lowe, G.R. 103
    Merl Inc. 103-106
    Midwest Aircraft Instruments 9
    Miller Air Sports 18
    Quam-Nichols Co. 99
    Sky Sales..25
    Thompson Associates 9
Svendsen, Jon ....18, 26 ff.
Tachometer
    electric, troubleshooting 65
    hourmeter 66
    hourmeter removal 67
    hourmeter, drum setting 67
    hourmeter, reinstallation 68
    maintenance 63-70
    maintenance, logging 66, 69
    mechanical, construction 66
    mechanical, disassembly 66
    mechanical, reinstallation 68
    mechanical, removal..66
    mechanical, repair techniques 66-70
    repair, FAA policy 66
    tach-generators...65
Thompson Associates 9
Tools
    ball peen hammer 69
    battery hydrometer ....145 ff., 168
    Baumanometer 54
    belt tension gauge 124
    burnishing tool 111
    connector receptacle 84
    flashlight 4
    growler ....131 ff.
    hot-light ....117 ff.
    instrument panel renovation ....4 ff.
    nut drivers 4

Tools, continued
    ohmmeter 4, 108, 116
    oscilloscope ....119 ff.
    peak-to-peak voltmeter ....119 ff.
    pliers, diagonal...4
    pliers, needlenose 4, 69
    pliers, terminal connector 83
    portable floodlight 4
    putty knife..4
    ratchet set 4
    resistance probe 83
    safety goggles 4
    screwdriver, Phillips 4, 97
    screwdrivers 83
    Support Systems Analyzer ....121 ff.
    Swiss army knife 104
    test lamp 130
    test points 130
    thread tap 86
    trouble-light...4
    wrench, Allen...4 ff., 7
    wrench, open-end 4
    wrench, socket..83
Trade-a-Plane 22
Turbine inlet temperature (TIT) with EGT 79
Type Certificate Data Sheet, gauge markings indicated 9
Vacuum pumps
    design and operation ....39 ff.
    dry vs. wet 32
    location 31
Vacuum pump maintenance
    Airborne ....39 ff.
    Airborne 343 Test Kit 47
    Airborne Pneumatic Source Indicator 46
    causes of failure ....39 ff.
    detecting imminent failure 45
    drive misalignment 41
    Edo (Sigma-Tec) ....39 ff.
    failure, FAA warning 39
    failures due to normal wear 44

Vacuum pump maintenance, continued
  failures due to rapid acceleration 43
  failures due to rough handling 43
  foreign object ingestion 41
  heat and altitude stress 42
  longevity 44
  NTSB and FAA concerns 39
  overspeeding 42
  preflight checks 45
  pump lugging 44
  replacement 47-49
  reverse rotation 43
  solvent contamination 41
  standby pumps 46
  suction gauge failure warnings 46
  tested by Pamco Industries 42
Vacuum system maintenance
  (also see Air-oil separator) 32
  air filters 49
  air-oil separator 32
  FAA on air filters 49
  FAA rule on air-oil separator 38
  filter replacement 33
  filter replacement intervals 33
  valve screen cleaning 37
  valve screen cleaning, FAA permission 37
Vacuum systems
  central air filter 32
  design and operation 31
  effects of tobacco smoke 34
  relief valve function 37
  suction gauge indications 35
  suction lines 32
  suction relief valve 32
  system maintenance 31-35
  troubleshooting 39
  vacuum gauge 32
  vacuum pump 32
  value of heated air 35
  venturi, location 31

Voltage regulator
    (also see Battery maintenance) 135
    (also see Generator maintenance) 135-142
    adjustment for battery longevity 157
    construction and operation 136
    current regulator .... 137 ff.
    cutout relay design and operation 135
    evolution 135
    polarity 139
    principles of operation 135-137
    resistors 138
    temperature compensation 138
Voltage regulator maintenance
    air gap setting .... 141 ff.
    cleaning contact points 140
    general precautions 139
    voltage setting 140
    voltage setting, fixed resistance method 141
    variable resistance method 141
Weir, Jim .... 108 ff.
Willard W-78M battery, affected by AD 79-07-02 148
Window maintenance
    3M Strip Calk 90
    during panel refashioning 21
    leak protection 90
Youngquist, John 80
Zompolas, Thomas 43